Shrop

An Archaeological Guide

Michael Watson

Shropshire Books

Front cover: Caer Caradoc (Chapel Lawn) CPAT 87-C-4
Back Cover: Column Base from Forum colonnade, Wroxeter Roman City,
Michael Watson

© Michael Watson 2002
ISBN: 0-903802-80-5
Cover and book design by The Graphic Terrace: 01952 243395
Managing Editor: Helen Sample
Published by Shropshire Books,
the publishing imprint of Shropshire County Council's
Community and Environment Department
Printed in Great Britain by Livesey Limited

About the Author

Michael Watson was born and grew up in Sheffield.

He has lived and worked in Shropshire for over twenty years. He is currently Head of Archaeology for Shropshire County Council.

Acknowledgements

The publishers would like to thank the Clwyd-Powys Archaeological Trust for their permission to reproduce the following photographs in this book:

Stiperstones	93-C-586	p.15
The Berth	84-C-215	p.18
Black Knoll	95-C-1813	p.19
Bury Ditches	83-C-598	p.22
Caer Caradoc (Chapel Lawn)	87-C-4	p.23
Caer Caradoc (Church Stretton)	84-C-489	p.25
Nordy Bank	95-C-1775	p.30
Old Oswestry	95-C-1041	p.31

All other photographs in the book were taken by the author.

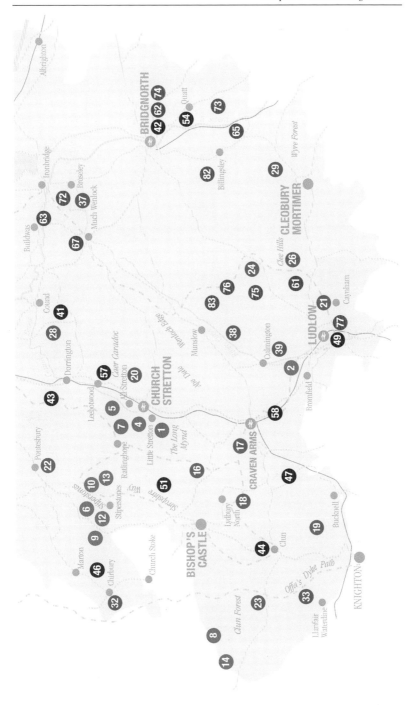

Abbreviations and Symbols

E	east
EH	English Heritage
ha	hectare
km	Kilometre
l, lhs	left, left hand side
m	metre
N	north
r, rhs	right, right hand side
S	south
W	west
(*)	site subject to restricted opening hours

Contents

Roman and Anglo-Saxon **35**

Castles **51**

The Medieval Church **73**

Medieval Town and Country **91**

Further Reading **105**

Glossary **106**

Introduction

This book is intended as an aid for those who wish to experience and enjoy at first hand the archaeological monuments of Shropshire. It aims to provide sufficient information for the selected sites to be located and visited, to describe their principal visible remains, and to place those remains in their archaeological and historical context.

The chronological range covered spans prehistory through to c.1500 AD, and a broadly chronological approach has been adopted for the gazetteer format. Individual site entries are grouped into period based chapters, with each preceded by a brief introductory discussion of the monument types. The chapters are arranged in chronological order.

When dealing with a county as well endowed with high quality archaeological remains as Shropshire, selectivity is essential. A number of criteria have been used for selecting the entries for inclusion: Firstly, on a general level, an attempt has been made to choose a broad representative sample of the major monument classes for each of the periods covered. For the sake of brevity parishes churches and vernacular architecture have been excluded from the medieval section. Secondly, much emphasis has been placed on those monuments which are well preserved, visually interesting and impressive. Accessibility has been another crucial consideration, with preference given to those sites which have some form of public access, even if only visual. Finally, the writer's own personal preferences have inevitably, and deliberately, been a major influence. Undoubtedly, some people will be disappointed at the exclusion of particular monuments, perhaps personal favourites, or their local site. Most of the old war-horses have made it however, as well as, it is hoped, some less well known but equally rewarding sites to visit.

All site entries have a standard format. Firstly, each monument is numbered so that it can be located on the map. Then the site name is given, followed by an indication of the broad date of the visible remains. Next is the National Grid Reference (e.g. SJ 620105). Locational details follow; firstly in relation to the distance of the site from the nearest Shropshire town (as crows fly), then more local directions. The directions are designed to be used with Ordnance Survey maps to locate the various sites. Ordnance Survey 1:25,000 maps are recommended as these show public footpaths and all field boundaries.

An asterisk (*) indicates that the site is subject to restricted opening hours. 'EH' denotes a property managed by English Heritage, who should be contacted for information on their monument opening times. Unless otherwise indicated, assume the site is accessible at any reasonable time.

It must be stressed that while most of the monuments included have been chosen because of their accessibility, this does not mean there is a presumption of general public access to each. Where sites are either crossed or lie adjacent to public rights of way, the access, physical or visual, is restricted to that right of way. If further, more general access is required then the landowner's permission should be sought beforehand wherever possible.

Although efforts have been made to check that the accessibility of monuments is as described, it must be borne in mind that circumstances can change, and even public footpaths can be altered. No liability can be accepted for any errors in the information provided.

Bronze Age

The earliest man-made remains that survive in the Shropshire landscape belong to the period of British prehistory known as the Bronze Age, spanning the period c.2400-700 BC. The most conspicuous and numerous class of monument of this era is the circular burial mound of earth or stone and usually covering single or occasionally multiple burials. They largely date to the early Bronze Age (c.2400-1400 BC). When constructed of earth these mounds are known as barrows, and most would have originally been surrounded by a quarry ditch. The vast majority of Shropshire examples are simple bowl barrows, so called after their distinctive profile and form that punctuate so many skylines. A rare example of a more elaborate type of barrow is the Shooting Box Barrow on the Long Mynd. This is a disc barrow - a central mound on a wide platform surrounded by a ditch and outer bank.

In upland areas, in particular, the fabric of the burial mound is often built of stones, and in this case they are called cairns, as for instance the examples on the Stiperstones. Both barrows and cairns can occur either in isolation or grouped in cemeteries, like at Bromfield, and they frequently served as a focus for later burials.

A related type of monument is the ring-cairn, comprising a circular bank of stones usually enclosing a hollow central area. They are broadly contemporary with round barrows and cairns, and are thought to be ritual monuments. The nature of these rituals is unclear, though they are likely to be associated with the burials that are commonly found within them.

To this same general early Bronze Age period can be assigned the county's two stone circles. These enigmatic monuments are frequently found in association with contemporary funerary monuments, as indeed is the case with the Shropshire examples. Clearly of considerable ritual and ceremonial importance, they may also have served as communal gathering points. Some perhaps were used to chart the passage of time through their alignment on the movement of heavenly bodies.

The local communities who created this abundance of funerary and ceremonial monuments were also responsible for developing an even more structured and ordered landscape. In Shropshire this is evidenced by a series of linear earthworks in the south-west uplands, known as cross-ridge dykes. These earthworks, consisting of one or more banks and ditches running parallel to each other, cut across ridges and projecting spurs of land. They are likely to have functioned as territorial boundaries, and perhaps in the case of the Long Mynd examples, served to delimit and control access to and from different areas of land usage. Most cross-ridge dykes date from the period c.1400 BC onwards, and this is consistent with the date from the Devil's Mouth Dyke example.

1. BARRISTERS PLAIN CROSS-RIDGE DYKE, LONG MYND
2nd millennium BC

SO 426927. 3km SW of Church Stretton. Take Burway Road E from Church Stretton to the Long Mynd. After 3km take left turn at road fork (sign-posted Asterton). Continue for 1.5km to Pole Cottage. 250m further along road take footpath (signposted Little Stretton) SE across open moorland for 1.5km.

The cross-ridge dyke runs SW to NE, almost straight for 170m across the narrowest point of a projecting ridge between Grindle Hill to the SE and Round Hill to the NW. The heather-covered bank averages 5.5m wide and 0.6m high and is fronted along its west side by a continuous 3m wide ditch. Both bank and ditch fade and terminate at the head of the steep slopes either end of the ridge. There is a 4m wide gap c.60m from the SE end, possibly original, which coincides with a trackway along the ridge. The dyke serves to cut off the spur of Grindle Hill from the main plateau of the Long Mynd by creating an effective barrier to access from the west.

2. BROMFIELD BARROWS
2nd millennium BC

SO 489778. 3km NW of Ludlow. Turn N off A49 at Bromfield, cross the railway line, after 300m take minor road to left, 1st barrow 120m ahead on rhs of the road.

The complex of archaeological monuments at Bromfield covering over four millennia has led to the area justly being claimed as the foremost rural archaeological site in the (Welsh) border. Visually, it is the Bronze Age monuments that dominate this sequence. On a level gravel terrace between the rivers Onny, Teme and Corve once stood over twenty barrows and at least three associated flat cremation cemeteries. Together these Bronze Age funerary monuments span the period c.2000-900 BC. Only three of the barrows still survive as substantial upstanding monuments.

Robin Hood's Butt barrow (SO 489778) stands at the end of a low ridge overlooking Ludlow golf course. Visitors should beware the occasional flying golf ball. The barrow is a large and impressive monument, 28m in diameter, steep-sided and over 4m high. Cremated bones of a boy and a bronze implement were found 3m below the mound top during its excavation in 1884. It was the planting of the tree that still crowns the mound summit that prompted the excavation.

800m to the SE alongside the B4365 road is another splendid barrow (SO 496773). A somewhat incongruous setting, in the middle of a golf course, wedged between a road and racecourse, in no way detracts from its impact.

The tree on the summit of the 3.5m high mound, as at the previous barrow, was planted in 1884 following the excavation. The old excavation trench is still visible on the N side of the mound. An oval stone-lined cist containing cremated bones was found at the base of the mound. A secondary cremation burial within an urn was also located 0.6m below the mound top.

The third and largest barrow is (SO 497770) clearly visible within the field 300m to the SE in the angle between the B4365 and the railway line. Though much reduced by ploughing it stands out as a well defined 50m diameter mound, up to 1.7m high. It remains unexcavated.

Bromfield Barrow (No. 2)

3. CARREG-Y-BIG STANDING STONE
2nd millennium BC

SJ 256328. 4km NW of Oswestry. From Oswestry take B4580 W for 3.5km then take road N to Carreg-y-Big. Continue on road NE (marked Selattyn) for 700m. Public Footpath on lhs of road crosses field to stile. Go over stile and stone is visible 50m to the N at junction of three field boundaries.

It is presumably this fine standing stone that is commemorated in the

name of the nearby farm, Carreg-y-Big - 'the big stone'. The stone itself occupies what must originally have been a conspicuous position midway up the S facing hill slope of a small valley. Perhaps it served as a way-marker to travellers along the valley route still followed today by the modern road. The stone, which leans markedly to the W is a large block of the locally out-cropping carboniferous limestone. It stands an impressive 2m high, is 1.2m wide and 1m deep, and has an uncommonly smooth S face. Traces of stone packing can be seen around the base. A stone fragment lying close by may formerly have been attached to the stone's top.

Carreg-y-Big standing stone

4. DEVIL'S MOUTH CROSS-RIDGE DYKE, LONG MYND
2nd millennium BC

SO 439943. 1km W of Church Stretton. Take the Burway road leading W from Church Stretton to the Long Mynd. The road bisects the earthwork.

Breathtakingly sited across the evocatively named Devil's Mouth - a saddle on an eastward projecting spur of the Long Mynd between Cardingmill Valley to the N and Townbrook Valley to the S. This fine cross-ridge dyke extends for c.140m, though a central stretch of c.35m is now missing where it is crossed by the Burway Road and an area of former car parking. Both ends terminate where the precipitous slopes render it unnecessary. It comprises a stone and earth bank, up to 6m wide and 1.5m high in the southern portion, with shallow flanking ditches to either side; that to the W being the larger. The N half is less well preserved, but still clearly visible as a 4m wide bank standing nearly a metre high on its west side also flanked only on this side by a single ditch. A radiocarbon date of c.1500-1300 BC from the dyke places its construction firmly in the Bronze Age.

Any defensive role for the dyke can surely be discounted as it is overlooked by higher ground on both sides of the saddle that it straddles. Its purpose was probably to control access along the ancient east-west route across the Long Mynd. A route perpetuated today, 3,500 years later by the Burway.

Devil's Mouth Cross-Ridge Dyke

5. HIGH PARK CROSS-RIDGE DYKE, LONG MYND
2nd millennium BC

SO 443967. 3km N of Church Stretton. Take the minor road NW from All Stretton sign-posted High Park. After 2km park just before cattle grid and then follow bridleway W uphill. The earthwork is crossed after 600m.

At 380m in length, the most extensive of the Long Mynd cross-ridge dykes, it traverses a broad ridge between hollows to its N and S, fading out as the crest of the natural slopes are approached. The N third lies in enclosed pasture and survives as a 6m wide bank, up to 0.8m high and surmounted by a modern hedge. No ditch is visible here, though cropmark evidence confirms its former existence flanking the W side of the bank. A ditch is, however, clearly evident in the greater portion of the earthwork in the moorland area, where it averages 5m wide and 0.6m deep. It fronts the W side of the bank, which stands up to 1.2m high on the W up-slope side and some 8m wide. A trackway breaches the dyke at the junction of the pasture and moorland zones and immediately south of this a subsidiary bank, low and narrow, runs parallel to the main rampart for c.70m. This apparent strengthening of the earthwork at this point may indicate that the current gap is an original one and the trackway therefore of some antiquity. The dyke would have barred passage from W to E along the ridge.

High Park Cross-Ridge Dyke

6. HOARSTONES STONE CIRCLE
2nd millennium BC

Hoarstones Stone Circle

SO 324999. 1.5km NW of Shelve. From the A488 at Shelve cross-roads take the road N to Hemford for 1km. Turn left to end of minor road, then follow path E along hedgeline for 300m. Monument in centre of field ahead.

The Hoarstone Circle, sometimes, also known as the Marsh Pool or Blackmarsh Circle, is situated on flat, often waterlogged ground near the northern end of Stapeley Hill. It stands close to the junction of three ancient parish boundaries; hence the name 'Hoarstone' or 'boundary stone'. Like many stone circles this one is more properly described as oval or egg-shaped, with diameters at 23 and 20 metres. It is made up of 37 small closely set stones, mostly less than knee high and all of local dolerite stone. A single unshaped boulder 1m high stands in the middle of the ring, slightly S of its centre.

Thin cylindrical holes can be seen drilled into the inner faces of two stones. These have been interpreted as of significance due to their position in relation to the major axes of the circle. However, a 19th century source relates how they were made by local lead miners who filled them with gunpowder to fire as "stone guns" in celebration of local weddings. Thankfully, our source reports, "it is satisfactory to know that the miners suffer more from them than the stones do".

Detailed surveys of the site have also led to claims that three gaps in the circle are original and of significance, in that, from the central stone, they align with the peaks of Bromlow Callow, Stiperstones and Corndon Hill, three prominent features on the surrounding skyline. Immediately to the north-west of the circle two small, low, turf-covered round mounds are probably associated Bronzes Age burial cairns. Neither circle nor barrows have been excavated.

7. LONG MYND BARROWS
2nd millennium BC

SO 421953-430960. 3.5km NW of Church Stretton. Take Burway road W from Church Stretton to the Long Mynd. After c.3km take right turn at road fork (Signposted Ratlinghope). Continue for 1km to car park on rhs of road. The first barrow lies immediately to the N.

Over twenty prehistoric barrows and cairns pepper the high plateau landscape of the Long Mynd, a testament to the extent of exploitation of these upland areas during the Bronze Age. A particularly fine series of these monuments are located at the northern end of the Mynd, where they lie alongside the ancient trackway known as the Portway, itself probably prehistoric in origin.

The first of these is the Shooting Box barrow so named after a grouse shooting hut which, until its removal in 1992, stood inserted into the barrow mound. This barrow is the only known Shropshire example of a disc barrow. The prominent green grassed central mound is 21m in diameter, and up to 2.3m high. It sits centrally within a flat circular enclosure of 54m across and defined by a low concentric bank. The heather covered 5m wide bank is clearly visible except in the north-east segment where it is cut through in two places by a modern track. A hollow on the N side of the mound is where the Shooting Box stood. Analysis of a soil layer sealed beneath the barrow has indicated a landscape of open grassland immediately prior to the erection of the barrow and dated to c.1950-1700 BC.

200m to the NE beside the Portway track stands another barrow (SO 423965), 28m across and 6m high. Its bowl-shaped profile stands out clearly against the skyline. A hollow in the top of the mound is likely to be the result of an unrecorded antiquarian investigation. Follow the track for a further 1km till it veers to the left and crosses the minor road. Ahead on the crest of Duckley Nap is the first of two barrows called Robin Hood's Butts (SO 430960). It is large and impressive, 36m in diameter and 4m high. It has a most unusual stepped profile, giving it the appearance of a smaller upper mound on top of a flat topped larger mound. An old field bank crosses the lower N side of the barrow, beyond which lies an area of enclosed grassland and into which the base of the mound extends. It was probably this barrow that the antiquarian Hartshorne referred to in 1841 as having been "opened" a few years earlier, when "nothing was discovered". From the summit of the mound the other barrow is clearly visible some 50m to the N in the adjacent pasture land. It is a circular mound 21m across though somewhat flattened by ploughing and reduced in height to c.1.5m. A shallow depression up to 4m wide partially survives at the base of the mound and is a probable remnant of the original surrounding quarry ditch.

If you are fortunate enough to visit on a clear day, then marvel at the vistas northward, as no doubt the Bronze Age builders of these monuments did some 4000 years ago. Closer to hand, 500m to the SE, the familiar profile of yet another barrow can be seen silhouetted against the skyline.

Robin Hoods Butts barrows profiled on the horizon

8. LOWER SHORT DITCH
2nd millennium BC

SO 222880. 10km NW of Clun. From Mainstone take road W for 3.5km to Two Crosses road junction. From here take road marked 'Unsuitable for motors' NW for 2 km. Earthwork visible from road.

This is the easternmost of two linear earthworks that span the Kerry Ridgeway and also the Shropshire-Wales border. Cyril Fox in his seminal study of Offa's Dyke considered it and a number of similar earthworks to have been built by local Anglo-Saxon communities in the period prior to the erection of Offa's Dyke. More recently they have been interpreted as medieval territorial boundaries. However in form and siting they have much in common with cross-ridge dykes of prehistoric date. In the absence therefore of firm evidence to the contrary they are assumed here to be of probable Bronze Age date like the examples on the Long Mynd.

The Lower Short Ditch consists throughout of a single bank, 6m wide and up to 1.5m high, flanked along its W side by a continuous ditch 4m wide and 1m deep. It follows a straight course in a N-S direction for 750m, terminating at both ends at the head of steep dingles. Close to its N end the earthwork is crossed by the Kerry Ridgeway track. This ancient route is likely to have been in use since prehistory, and the earthwork is sited so as best to control movement along it. S of the ridgeway intersection a modern road runs along the top of

the bank for a length of 400m. Beyond this the southernmost 300m length has recently been cleared of its blanketing shroud of conifer plantation. Here at least, a better appreciation can be had of the earthworks original form.

Lower Short Ditch

9. MITCHELL'S FOLD STONE CIRCLE
2nd millennium BC

SO 304983. 9km N of Bishop's Castle. From the A488 at White Grit cross-roads follow the signs to Mitchell's Fold stone circle along road to W for 2.5km till reaching track leading off the road at a sharp bend. Drive 400m along track to small car parking area. Walk across cattle grid, follow track for 300m to stone circle. EH

Perched high in a bleak and exposed position on the long ridge-top of Stapeley Hill, Mitchell's Fold can rightly lay claim to being the best known and most evocative of all the county's prehistoric monuments. From it, marvellous views are to be had across the Shropshire hills and westwards into Wales - its builders chose the site well. The circle of stones, slightly elliptical in shape, is 27m across, and originally consisted of some thirty stones, though only fifteen now survive. None seem to have been shaped or dressed, and all are of the local dolerite stone. Most of the surviving stones stand less than a metre high, while some are mere stumps at turf level, but the tallest is almost 2m high.

Mitchell's Fold Stone Circle

Closer inspection reveals a series of narrow cultivation ridges running E-W through the circle and to either side of it. These ridges cover large areas of Stapeley Hill, but both their date and their relationship to the stone circle remain uncertain.

Some 90m to the SE are the denuded remains of a round cairn, and immediately next to this a small squat standing stone on a slight prominence. This stone has the appearance of being in alignment with the stone circle and the summit of the brooding mass of Corndon Hill, 1.5km to the S - itself peppered with Bronze Age burial cairns. The lower S flanks of the hill were exploited in the Early Bronze Age for a particular type of volcanic rock (picrite) which outcrops here. This was used for the production of perforated shaft-hole axes. It was perhaps the trade generated by this industry that accounts for the plethora of Bronze Age monuments in the area.

Local folklore tells how long ago a magic cow on Stapeley Hill gave milk to all good folk of the neighbourhood, until an evil witch called Mitchell milked her into a sieve until dry, whereupon the cow disappeared never to return. As punishment the witch was turned into stone and a circle of stones erected to keep her in. Could this fable indicate there was once a central stone in the circle? Whatever, it is a fine tale worthy of a fine monument.

10. PENNERLEY BARROWS
2nd millennium BC

SO 349993. 11km NE of Bishops Castle. From Shelve head E along road to Pennerley for 500m. At a sharp bend take the footpath E for 700m to the top of Round Hill. Barrows visible from footpath which runs alongside adjacent field boundaries.

Two fine barrows inter-visible and situated within 200m of each other. They lie on and near the summit of Round Hill, both commanding extensive views eastwards in all directions. On approaching from the W the distinctive domed profile of the first barrow stands out clearly against the skyline and the dramatic backdrop of the Stiperstones. It is a particularly fine and well preserved example, standing an impressive 3m high and with a diameter of some 30m. There is no trace of any ditch surrounding the base of the turf covered mound.

Straight ahead to the E on top of a low narrow ridge is the second barrow, known fittingly as The Knapp. Topped by a stand of pine trees it lies in the angle of a field and adjacent to a small quaint cottage built into the lee of the E slopes of the ridge. The partially gorse-covered mound looks considerably higher when viewed from the W due to its siting on the crest of the ridge. The top of the mound has been dug into, creating a hollowed out platform. On the base of the hollow in its centre is a stone slab, possibly part of a cist from a secondary burial that would have been inserted into the mound. A small low mound immediately to the N of the barrow is probably a natural feature.

Pennerley Barrow

11. SELATTYN HILL RING CAIRN AND TOWER
2nd millennium BC

Sellatyn Hill Ring Cairn

SJ 256341. 1 km W of Selattyn. Take B4579 NW from Selattyn. After 1km take steep track on left. Follow sign for Selattyn Hill along woodland edge, then path across open fields to hill summit, where tower and cairn are signposted.

Within a clearing on the conifer planted summit of Selattyn Hill stand two monuments - physically together, yet separated in time by some 4,000 years. Of these the visitor will first notice a ruinous square tower, built in 1847 as a belvedere from which panoramic views of up to 100km distance could be enjoyed. As a vantage point the tower also saw service during World War II when it was used as a look-out post by the local Home Guard.

The tower stands within a Bronze Age ring cairn, just to the S of its centre. The cairn comprises a low unrevetted bank up to 3m wide, and consisting of large rounded boulders. It originally enclosed a flat open area of c.20m diameter which was surfaced by a spread of large rounded stones. Sherds of Early Bronze Age pottery and fragments of cremated bone were recovered from amongst these interior stones during an excavation in 1998. A gap in the bank on its SW side may be an original entranceway or possibly the result of later damage. Piles of stone debris from the tower now lie spread across the cairn.

Mr Crewe, a local landowner, had the tower built in commemoration of Prince Gwen, a supposed 6th century British prince who according to local folklore was killed in a battle fought at the nearby Morlas Brook. Mr Crewe presumably believed that the cairn was Gwen's burial place. He no doubt felt vindicated when during the building

of the tower "twelve urns, each containing burnt bones" were apparently found. Sadly, the eventual fate of these (presumably) Bronze Age urns and cremation burials is unknown.

12. STAPELEY HILL CAIRN
2nd millennium BC

Stapeley Hill Cairn

SO 312990. 10km N of Bishop's Castle. Follow directions as for Mitchell's Fold stone circle (p.10). The cairn is situated 1km NE of stone circle on top of narrow ridge on E side of Stapeley Hill, 150m N of modern cairn.

What this charming little cairn lacks in scale it more than makes up for in siting. From its position on the heights of Stapeley Hill, the faraway peaks of Cader Idris and Plynlimon can be seen on a clear day. The monument, 14m across, has the appearance of a ring

cairn with a circular bank of stones, 1.5m wide, around its circumference. Within the ring is a low turf-covered stony mound c.7m across, and a scattering of angular stone blocks. The apparent ring-cairn form of this monument may be the chance result of stone robbing of an originally simple round cairn mound.

The cultivation ridges so evident over much of Stapeley Hill extend to surround this cairn. Despite detailed survey it has not been possible to establish the relationship between the two.

The ridges are at their most pronounced along the slopes of this narrow ridge-top where they are aligned across the contours on both sides of the ridge. Occasional rows of protruding stones run parallel to these ridges, perhaps originally serving to subdivide areas of cultivation. Although these linear features are undoubtedly the remnants of a former arable field system, they exhibit none of the characteristics of medieval ridge-and-furrow. Their date is unknown, but there is a possibility that they are of prehistoric origin.

13. STIPERSTONES CAIRNS
2nd millennium BC

SO 367984-368988. 10km NE of Bishop's Castle. Best approached from the Stiperstones car park (SO 369977). Public footpath (signposted) leads N from car park up to, and along Stiperstones ridge.

Worth a journey for the views alone. The dramatic Stiperstones ridge with its projecting tors and scree-strewn slopes bears the remains of a cairn cemetery spread along its spine. When ascending the ridge from the S the first cairn encountered (SO 36739848) lies some 150m S of Manstone Rock. It occupies the peak of a projecting natural rock stack and is visible as a 12m diameter round cairn of stones whose body of angular quartzite blocks stands over 1m high. A small circular

Largest of the Stiperstones cairns (foreground) CPAT 93-C-586

hollowed out modern cairn stands in the middle of its prehistoric predecessor.

A second cairn lies c.50m to the NW (SO 36789852). In form it is a ring-cairn, oval in shape, measuring 10m x 8.5m, and encircles a natural stone outcrop. Its ring bank is of stone rubble construction c.1.5m in width, and is somewhat flattened along its south-west segment. The next outcropping rock tor is Manstone Rock, surmounted by its OS trig. Pillar. 40m to the NE of this rock base is a small partially turf-covered cairn, 5m in diameter and 0.5m high.

The finest of all the Stiperstones cairns is the most northerly of the group (SO 36799879), alongside the path leading to the Devil's Chair rock outcrop. An island of bare stones gleaming in a wine-dark sea of heather; this great cairn stands 1.7m high and 24m in diameter. Its flat top is surmounted in the N half by a smaller and probably relatively modern cairn, hollowed out to form a shooting butt. The base of this hollow has exposed a large natural boulder over which the prehistoric cairn was apparently built. The S half of the cairn has a hummocky appearance due to disturbance.

Warning - visitors on the 21 December, beware, for all the ghosts of Shropshire are reputed to meet at the Stiperstones on this day. If that is not enough, then watch out for the "Seven Whistlers": Legend has it that six birds fly up and down the Stiperstones slopes looking for a lost companion. When the seventh bird is found, the end of the world will occur - scary.

14. UPPER SHORT DITCH
2nd millennium BC

SO 192876. 12km NW of Clun. From Clun take B4368 to Anchor. At Anchor Inn road junction take minor road NE for 2km to junction with Kerry Ridgeway track. Follow ridgeway track E for 800m. Monument visible from track.

Like its counterpart the Lower Short Ditch, 3km to the E, this earthwork straddles the Kerry Ridgeway, which here forms the boundary with Wales. To the N of the ridgeway track the Welsh section of the earthwork can be seen cutting a broad swathe through a conifer plantation. The Shropshire length to the S is clearly visible as it runs through pasture land for a distance of 350m before ending at a field boundary. It probably once extended further S to terminate, like its N end, at the head of a steep natural valley slope in typical cross-dyke fashion. Perhaps originally some 900m in length it would have spanned the entirety of the ridge, crossing at a point on the lower down-slope of gently W sloping ground. The earthwork survives as a 1.5m high bank, partly gorse-clad and surmounted by a field boundary on its E side. A continuous ditch fronts its W side. Both its scale and siting rule against the earthwork ever having had a truly defensive function. Control of access along this important ancient E-W routeway must surely have been its primary role.

Iron Age

In contrast to the preceding Bronze Age it is settlement sites that dominate the archaeology of Shropshire during the Iron Age period (c.700 BC-43 AD). Of these the most spectacular are the hillforts, of which there are over fifty in the county. These impressive monuments, with their massive ramparts and ditches dominate the surrounding landscape from their elevated positions. Hillforts are defended settlements, usually sited on a hill top, ridge-end or plateau edge. Occasionally they can be found on low ground, as at the Berth, but even then deliberately sited with a view to commanding wide surrounding areas and utilising natural defensive features. Although the origins of some hillforts may lie in the later Bronze Age, most of the earthworks visible today are likely to date to the latter centuries of the Iron Age and in some cases be the culmination of centuries of development.

Shropshire hillforts display a remarkable diversity of size, shape and complexity. They range from relatively small forts of some 1.5 hectares to enormous strongholds like Titterstone Clee covering 28 hectares. Their defences likewise vary greatly from a single bank and ditch to multiple ranks of elaborate ramparts and ditches, as so spectacularly seen at Old Oswestry. Despite their frequently inhospitable locations, most hillforts are likely to have housed some form of permanent settlement, though the function of these settlements probably varied through both time and space.

During the 1st millennium BC not all people in Shropshire, however, lived in these hilltop fortresses. Indeed, probably the majority of the population lived in small defended farmsteads or unenclosed settlements, but such sites rarely survive in an above-ground form today. An exception is the settlement at Black Knoll on the southern slopes of the Long Mynd. The well preserved contemporary field system that surrounds this settlement is a reminder that agriculture formed the basis of life for most of these prehistoric communities.

15. THE BERTH
1st millennium BC

SJ 429237. 12km NW of Shrewsbury. The monument lies on private land 1.5km N of Baschurch. No public access, owners permission to visit should be sought.

Few Shropshire monuments have been the subject of such intense, and sometimes fantastical, historical speculation as the Berth. This has largely centred on whether it is the site of 'Pengwern' the legendary residence of Cynddylan, a reputed 7th century Prince of Powys. Regardless of the historical basis of these claims the archaeological evidence is emphatic - this is essentially a prehistoric monument. It is an unusual and curious example of an Iron Age fort, situated somewhat atypically in an area of low lying marshy ground.

It consists of two natural glacial mounds each enclosed and defended by a single rampart of stone and gravel. The larger enclosure had its rampart faced on the lower outer side by large stones. Access to it was through an inturned entrance on the E side, though this, along with some of the interior has been damaged by 19th century gravel digging. The much smaller enclosure 120m to the NE has traces of two possible mutilated entrances to the N and S. Both enclosures are linked by a raised causeway, and a further causeway 240m long connects them to the higher, drier ground to the south. It was while clearing out a cutting through this S causeway in 1906 that a bronze cauldron, probably of late Iron Age date, was found.

Despite its low-lying position the Berth must have been a place of considerable natural strength, for both of the fortified mounds were

The Berth CPAT 84-C-215

formerly islands within an extensive mere, of which Berth Pool, immediately S of the main mound, is the sole shrunken remnant. Limited excavations in 1962-3 provided evidence for three distinct phases of occupation spanning the middle to late Iron Age and Roman periods. Analysis of the sediments of Berth Pool has also demonstrated that continuous widespread woodland clearance occurred in the environs from the late Bronze Age through to the mid/late Iron Age.

16. BLACK KNOLL, LONG MYND, SETTLEMENT AND FIELD SYSTEM
1st millennium BC/early 1st millennium AD

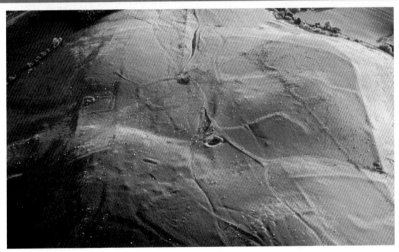

Black Knoll settlement and field system CPAT 95-C-1813

SO 389878. 6km E of Bishop's Castle. Fortunately the Shropshire Way path runs straight through these earthworks. From the S, access the path from the minor road to Asterton, 400m N of its junction with A489. A steep 1/2km walk leads to the site.

On the S slopes of the Long Mynd overlooking the Onny valley above Plowden is one of the most remarkable earthwork complexes in Shropshire. It forms a truly palimpsest landscape, with its 32 hectares spanning two thousand years of usage of this tract of upland. The most extensive and impressive element is a late prehistoric/Roman period field system complete with a network of inter-linking trackways, and an associated nucleated settlement. The settlement earthworks occupy a S facing shelf, that would have offered some shelter on this exposed hill slope, and is close to a natural spring. Up to twelve rectangular and sub-circular platforms each representing probable house or building sites and some with associated courtyards, cluster together. It is of great importance as an example of the type of unenclosed settlement that so rarely survives in the archaeological record of this era.

Three major trackways in the form of hollow-ways radiate from the settlement. The Port Way, the ancient ridgeway route that traverses the spine of the Long Mynd, partially coincides with these. The network of fields that surround the settlement are connected to and therefore contemporary with the trackways. The fields themselves are formed by lynchets, in some places up to 3m high and incorporating natural terraces and rock outcrops. They produce a pattern of generally large irregular fields similar to the widespread so-called 'Celtic' field systems of southern England. At least two phases of field system are apparent, and so were clearly in use for a considerable period of time. Together, both fields and settlement provide

dramatic evidence for the arable exploitation of Shropshire's uplands by farming communities in prehistoric and Roman times.

Some 1,500 years later these same hill slopes were used again, this time for rabbit farming. Just W of the settlement earthworks a low embanked roughly circular enclosure, 65m across, is likely to be a post-medieval rabbit warren - though it was once thought to be prehistoric. Also belonging to the rabbit farming phase are a number of small rectangular pillow mounds scattered among the other earthworks. A hedged enclosure on the S down-slope is to this day called 'Warren House'. The climax of the prolonged and varied use of this hillside came in the late 19th century when it was incongruously employed as a golf course - see if you can disentangle the tees and greens from the other earthworks.

17. BURROW HILL CAMP
1st millennium BC

SO 382831. 4km W of Craven Arms. The site is best accessed via footpath from Aston on Clun.

The long and steep climb up Burrow Hill is at times trying, but a fine reward awaits the zealous. The multivallate pear shaped hillfort that adorns the summit is a gem. Four ranks of massive banks and ditches defend much of the perimeter. The exception is along the NW side where the hill slopes are the steepest,

for here there is a single rampart, ditch and counter-scarp bank. There are three original entrances. The main entrance at the NE is of an elaborate inturned design, further strengthened by having the inner rampart offset at an oblique angle to prevent direct access to the interior. Another strong entrance on the S side is approached via a causeway to a 30m long inturn on the inner rampart. The third entrance at the SW apex of the fort is in the form of a narrow passageway between the ramparts.

Evidence for an earlier and smaller hillfort survives in the form of a bank that cuts off the highest parts of the hill on its E and S sides. Entry to this enclosure was through a simple break in the rampart on the E side.

A notable feature of the fort interior, particularly in the SW and NW quadrants, is the existence of large numbers of round level platforms.

These are likely to be hut platforms. Excavation of one of these in 1978 was shown to carry the gullies and post-holes of at least two circular huts. The inhabitants of this hilltop stronghold would have been well provided with natural water sources as two springs rise within its defences; one, adjacent to the main NE entrance, and the other within a gap in the third rampart at the SE corner.

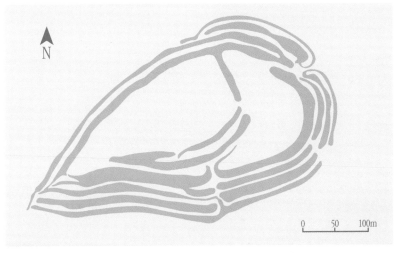

0   50   100m

Burrow Hill Camp

18. BURY DITCHES HILLFORT
1st millennium BC

SO 328837. 3.5km NE of Clun. Take B4363 E from Clun for 3km to Clunton, then minor road N (signposted) from Clunton for 2.5km till reaching Bury Ditches car park. Follow signed footpath from car park to hillfort.

When a severe winter storm in 1976 felled many of the trees on the summit

of Sunnyhill it revealed for the first time in decades one of the finest hillforts in Britain - Bury Ditches. Roughly oval in shape and enclosing an area of c.3ha, its awesome defences even today present an intimidating spectacle. Around its northern circuit where the natural hill slopes are less steep these defences comprise four, and at the NE up to five, successive ranks of steep profiled ramparts standing as much as 7m in height and each with an outer ditch. A series of hollows at the rear of the innermost rampart on the north side may mark the site of contemporary former structures or perhaps quarry scoops for the building of the rampart. On the S and E sides there are only two, though substantial, ramparts, with an intervening ditch - the steeper slopes on this side clearly being considered sufficient additional protection here.

Perhaps most impressive of all are two elaborate original entrances, one facing SW and the other NE. The former is a 'staggered entrance', fashioned by the N ramparts overlapping those curving from the S to create a deep and narrow 90m long passageway overlooked throughout its length from both sides. A protracted and bewildering killing ground for any would be assailants of the W gate. That at the NE is a classic example of an inturned entrance formed by the inner rampart and the second rampart on the N side, turning inwards on either side to create a passage extending 40m into the interior of the hillfort.

This outstanding complex of earthworks is likely to be the culmination of centuries of development during the later 1st millennium BC.

Bury Ditches CPAT 83-C-598

19. CAER CARADOC, CHAPEL LAWN
1st millennium BC

SO 310768. 5km S of Clun. From Clun take A488 S for 5km to New Invention, then road to Chapel Lawn E for 1.5km. At road junction take road W for 800m. From lhs of road, shortly after sharp bend, follow footpath across hillside parallel to field edge for c.700m, then short sharp ascent S to hilltop.

Caer Caradoc, Chapel Lawn CPAT 87-C-4

One of two Shropshire hillforts named after Caractacus, the legendary Catuvallaunian prince who led the British resistance against the Roman army till his defeat and capture in 52 AD. It is a superb earthwork, dominating the valley of the River Redlake from its elevated position. A roughly aubergine-shaped interior is enclosed on the N side by two banks and ditches, becoming three in the centre. On the S side there is a single rampart, ditch and counterscarp bank. There are two entrances to the fort, at the E and W ends, and both are inturned. The W approach to the fort is by far the easier along flatter ground and hence the W entrance is the more heavily defended. It is truly stupendous. Here, the widely spaced and voluptuously curving ramparts are huge, attaining a height of up to 7m above the base of the rock-cut ditch. S of the entrance a third bank and ditch enhances its defensive capability. So too do the slightly staggered ends of the ramparts at the entrance causeway, which prevent any direct approach to the gateway.

There were at least two phases in the construction of these defensive ramparts. The first consisted of dry stone wall faced ramparts built of flat siltstone flags. At a later date these dry-stone defences were heightened and widened by a dump construction rampart.

An inner quarry ditch with a distinctly scalloped edge skirts the interior perimeter. A number of shallow circular depressions, especially along the inside of the S rampart may indicate possible house sites, sheltering behind the earthwork on this exposed summit.

20. CAER CARADOC HILLFORT, CHURCH STRETTON
1st millennium BC

SO 477953. 2km NE of Church Stretton. Best approached from Willstone (SO 491953). Follow track W for 700m then take path NW, climbing hill slope and approaching Caer Caradoc summit from E.

On a scale of 10 this scores 11. Perched eyrie-like atop its lofty hog's-back volcanic ridge Caer Caradoc offers a sumptuous feast to those prehistorians with a penchant for majestic panoramas.

The hillfort straddles the hill summit, enclosing 3ha within ramparts that slavishly follow the landform's natural contours. The inner rampart is scarped out of the steep hill-slopes to stand up to 8m high externally while not exceeding 1.5m internally. It is continuous throughout its circuit except along the SE where it incorporates natural rock outcrops. A shallow probable quarry ditch, stepped in a sequence of scoops, flanks the inside of the rampart. An outer rampart surrounds much of the stronghold and this too has a quarry ditch alongside its inner face, with more of the distinctive hollow segments - possibly indicative of its excavation by gang working. The S approach to the hill summit is the least steep, hence at this one point there is a third defensive rampart across the isthmus. At the SE

Caer Caradoc hillfort, Church Stretton CPAT 84-C-489

angle is the sole original entrance - it is inturned, with a recessed guard chamber on the S side. From it a probable contemporary terraced trackway descends for 300m down the hill slope.

Despite the inhospitable and craggy interior of this fortress there is ample evidence for habitation in the form of numerous small terraces and building platforms in its SE quadrant. No temporary refuge this, but a permanent settlement made more congenial by a small spring-fed pond inside the NW angle of the defences. On a warm summers day sip its cool waters, relax, sit back and watch the buzzards glide along Stretton dale.

21. CAYNHAM CAMP HILLFORT
1st millennium BC

SO 545737. 2.5km SE of Ludlow. If approached from Caynham take path W from Caynham Church for 250m then NW along field edges for 500m; then path W leading directly to and across N part of monument.

This univallate hillfort occupies the domed summit of a low hill overlooking the narrow valley of the Ledyche Brook to the W and the Cay Brook to the N. It is roughly oval in plan and encloses c.4ha. The partially tree-clad defences are at their most impressive towards the E where the rampart stands over 5m high in places and fronted by a 4m wide ditch and counter-scarp bank. A deeply inturned narrow passage through the rampart at the SE corner represents the original main entrance into the fort. On its N side, where the natural hill slopes are the steepest, the defensive rampart is either slight or non-existent. A bank, 80m

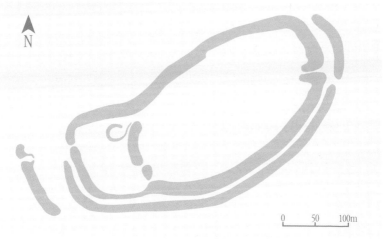

Caynham Camp hillfort

from the W end of the fort crosses the interior from N-S. This probably marks the position of the original W side of the fort which at a later date was extended W to create a rectangular shaped annexe forming the fort's W end. There are no vestiges of any original entrance through the W rampart into this annexe. A further annexe lies beyond, on the sloping ground below the W perimeter, defined by a single bank and with a possible original entrance through its NW corner.

Excavation has shown the earliest defences to have comprised a timber-laced rampart built c.390 BC. This was replaced first by a smaller, stone revetted bank, and later by the massive rampart visible today. Evidence for occupation was provided by an abundance of post-holes within the interior, and also an unusual semi-circular structure. This contrasted markedly with the paucity of artefacts found.

22. EARL'S HILL HILLFORT
1st millennium BC

SJ 409048. 1km SE of Pontesbury. From the A488 at Pontesford take minor road S (signposted Pontesford Hill). After 600m there is a small parking area on the 1hs of road. From here take path up steep slope through forestry for 1km directly to hill summit.

This dramatically sited hillfort comprises a main enclosure, an annexe to the S and a series of outworks to the N. The main fortification encloses 1.2ha of the hilltop. A single rampart and ditch forms the defence on all but the E side where the natural slopes are at their most precipitous. There is a slight counter-scarp bank at the NW.

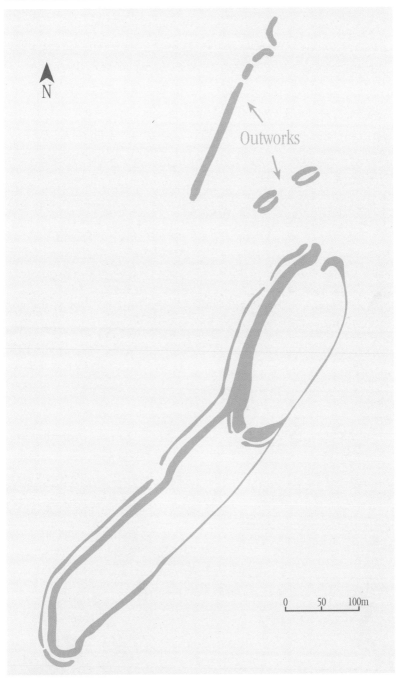

N

Outworks

0   50   100m

Earl's Hill hillfort

The main entrance is at the N end, and is unusual in that its E side is inturned while its W side is out-turned. Along the E side of the interior are a number of level areas abutting against rock outcrops, which may be building platforms. A simple gap in the rampart marks an entrance at the S end, where there is also a causeway across the ditch. This gives direct access into the S annexe - elongated and 1.6ha in extent. It is defended on the W and S by a scarp up to 6m high and an intermittent counter-scarp, supplemented by an outer ditch at the S corner. As with the main enclosure the natural slopes appear to have been considered ample protection on the E side.

90m N of the hillfort's N entrance are two 20m lengths of ditch with low banks on both sides. A further earthwork crosses the hill slope 70m beyond. It is a stout bank, 167m long, with an inturned entrance at its N end. These outworks may represent uncompleted outer defences to the hillfort proper.

Until the late 1800s Earl's Hill was the venue for popular festivities every Easter. These included a race down the hillside to the brook at its base. If the winner dipped the fourth finger of the right hand in the water it was said they would marry the first person of the opposite sex they met. Beats dating agencies.

23. FRON CAMP
1st millennium BC

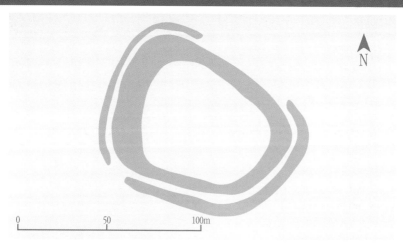

N

0   50   100m

Fron Camp

SO 250826. 5km W of Clun. On promontory overlooking Newcastle-on-Clun. From Newcastle church take track N up hillside, through gate and straight ahead across field. Turn left at field hedge and follow path uphill alongside hedge to summit.

Memorable views await those dedicated enough to make the steep ascent to Fron Camp. The spiritual rewards are instant, physical recovery may take a while longer. The earthwork is undated, though an Iron Age date is a good bet. As such, it represents perhaps the small defended settlement of a single family unit, and therefore provides an interesting counterbalance to the large communal hillforts that so dominate the region's archaeological record.

The site occupies a position of great strength on a knoll at the end of an elevated spur overlooking the Clun valley. It is roughly rectangular in shape though with somewhat rounded corners, and internally measures c.70 x 50m. The defences comprise a single surrounding outer ditch with a slight counter-scarp bank on the SE and SW sides, and an inner rampart. Both rampart and ditch are at their strongest on the less steep NW side. Elsewhere the precipitous natural slopes were clearly considered ample protection, for here, much of the rampart is reduced to an outward facing scarp. Ploughing has removed the ditch on the NE side, while tell-tale ridges also attest to ploughing of the domed interior at some time. The original entrance was probably at the SW corner where the ditch and bank are broken and the ground slightly hollowed. A pottery spindle whorl and several flint tools are reported from the site, other than these the visitor will have to exercise their imagination to people this slice of prehistoric landscape.

24. NORDY BANK HILLFORT
1st millennium BC

SO 575847. 11km NE of Ludlow. From Clee St Margaret take road N for 1km, on reaching crossroads take road E for c.400m. Park in layby and follow road straight ahead to gate and then path to Nordy Bank summit.

Nordy Bank is a roughly oval earthwork in a commanding position on the top of a spur off the lower W slopes of Brown Clee Hill. It is strongly defended by a single turf-covered rampart, up to 3m high in places, and an outer rock cut ditch together enclosing an area of c.3ha. The rampart is for the most part well preserved, but is breached in a number of places. Two of these gaps, one at the NE corner and on the S side, are original entrances. Though only 3m wide, both display the characteristic inward curve of ramparts to form slight inturned entrances. The inturns of the NE entrance have their ramparts widened, suggestive of having originally accommodated the regionally distinctive paired guard rooms.

The interior of the fort mirrors the sloping ground on which it is sited, giving it a terraced appearance, with the E up-slope area being markedly higher. Within the NW quadrant is a series of earthworks. The largest is a c.20m square low platform with a possible entrance on its E side. Its date and function are unclear. Abutting its SW corner is a small square ditched enclosure, just 6.5m across, which may

Nordy Bank CPAT 95-C-1775

be the site of a hut used by the Home Guard in WW II. Close by, to the W, are two small cairn-like mounds.

Nordy Bank is but one of three hillforts that formerly crowned the peaks of Brown Clee Hill. To the E the twin heights of Abdon Burf and Clee Burf were each topped by large hillforts. Both are now largely lost to quarrying, but which in its own way has created dramatic man-made landscapes on these hill summits.

25. OLD OSWESTRY HILLFORT
1st millenium BC

SJ 295310. On N edge of Oswestry town. Monument is signposted off B5069 road to Gobowen; from here follow Llwyn Road for 0.9km till reaching small roadside parking area on W side of monument. EH

Old Oswestry hillfort is big, bold and brassy. With good reason Cyril Fox described it as "the outstanding work of Early Iron Age type on the Marches of Wales". The complexity and scale of its defences more than compensate for its relatively low-lying position on a low glacial hill overlooking the Shropshire Plain to the N and E. A roughly diamond-shaped interior of c.6ha is enclosed by five ramparts and ditches for much of the perimeter, though these increase to an extraordinary seven on the W side. Access to the interior is gained by two heavily defended inturned entrances, facing E and W. That on the E has its entrance passageway flanked and overlooked by a bank on its S side.

It is the spectacular W entrance however, that dominates the whole site. Here a 20m wide sunken roadway ascends the hill slope protected lengthwise on either side by a flanking rampart. On either side of the roadway between the 3rd and 4th ramparts are a series of deep rectangular hollows divided by substantial banks. These are a feature unique to Old Oswestry. Many suggestions have been made as to their purpose, including water-tanks, stockpens, storage pits, quarries, or even an additional defensive feature to protect the entrance. Whatever their purpose they help to make the W entrance one of the most formidable of any hillfort in Britain.

Excavations in 1939-40 showed the hilltop to have been inhabited before the earthworks were built, probably during the late Bronze Age, and protected by a simple palisade. Thereafter, from c.600 BC onwards the defences were developed in successive stages of elaboration. This sequence began with a single stone-revetted box rampart which was added to by further circuits of defence. Finally, some time in the later Iron Age, the last phase of embellishment, which involved remodelling the great W entrance and building the present massive ramparts.

Standing at the base today and looking upwards, the serried ranks of ramparts present an intimidating and daunting spectacle. Prehistoric psychological warfare or an ostentatious statement of self-esteem? Perhaps both.

Old Oswestry CPAT 95-C-1041

26. TITTERSTONE CLEE, HILLFORT AND CAIRNS
2nd - 1st millennium BC

Titterstone Clee hillfort - the northern rampart

SO 594779. 7km NE of Ludlow. From A4117 take road signposted Clee Hill Summit for 2.5km. Park in disused quarry on S side of hill top. From here follow path signposted Shropshire Way up steep slope along narrow ridge between two quarries. Follow path till W summit is reached.

The distinctive landmark of Titterstone Clee with its white radar domes is archaeologically notable for being crowned by the largest of all Shropshire hillforts. Its univallate defensive circuit encloses a huge 28 hectares. Quarrying has destroyed much of the S defences, but along the N and E the rampart survives as a tumbled stone wall. It makes an impressive spectacle with its linear scree of angular dolerite blocks

following the contour around the hill summit. The Giant's Chair rock outcrop sits at the highest point on the W side of the hill. From its N flank the rampart runs N for 180m till reaching the original N entrance. This is 4m wide and slightly inturned. The rampart then heads SE and around the E end of the hill, where it is at its most impressive, up to 2.5m high and 13m wide. A series of four linear trenches can be seen at intervals across the rampart in this E section. These are the result of excavations undertaken in 1932, and which identified four phases of construction. Firstly, a timber-revetted earth rampart was built with timber entrances. After a period of disrepair the defences were then rebuilt in stone and the gateways remodelled, including two stone and timber guard rooms in the main SE entrance (now destroyed). Finally the defences were slighted. No dating evidence was forthcoming for any of these phases. Possible remains of internal structures, though also undated, were examined in 1991. Although essentially univallate, there is a short 30m length of double rampart on the sole surviving section of S defence where two grassed-over stony banks cross a narrow ridge between two old quarries.

The hilltop had been a place of meaning to local Bronze Age communities long before the heights were fortified. Two ring cairns on the W hill summit are evidence for this. The first, disturbed and only partially surviving is surmounted by a modern OS trig. pillar. What remains

of a central low mound is surrounded by the E arc of a stony ring bank, originally perhaps up to 28m in diameter. 80m to the SE, the other cairn is a low flat-topped circular mound of earth, 23m across, with remains of a stone kerb around its edge. The excavation trench of 1932 is still visible and this located a 2.3m deep circular pit beneath the centre of the mound, but no direct evidence for the monument's date. Its SW quadrant is truncated.

Until the mid 19th century the Titterstone Wake was held on the hill every last Sunday in August. Young women, "fine stand-up handsome wenches they were", would meet up with their menfolk and indulge in games such as the beguilingly named 'Kiss-in-the-ring'.

27. THE WREKIN HILLFORT
1st millennium BC

SJ 630082. 3km SW of Wellington. From M54 junction 7 take road to Little Wenlock S for 1.2km. Park in layby on lhs of road. Footpath to Wrekin signposted opposite through gate. Follow path to hill summit.

Like some monstrous beached whale the windswept Wrekin rises above the Severn Valley to be crowned by a hillfort often claimed as the tribal capital of the Cornovii in pre-Roman times. The fort comprises an inner enclosure of 3ha which defends the high central crest of the hill, and an outer enclosure of 8ha surrounding the lower slopes of the summit.

The inner enclosure has a main rampart that follows the crest of a steep slope which is partly artificially steepened at its base and with a slight counter-scarp bank. Inturned entrances are at the NE (Heaven Gate) and SW end, each with surface evidence for twin rectangular guard-chambers opening off the passageways. The rampart is at its most substantial where it crosses the hill to form the entrance works; elsewhere it survives only as a low mound. The outer ramparts are for the most part little more than terraces and utilise wherever possible natural rocky outcrops in their circuit. There are two of these terraces around much of the NE half of the site, and they

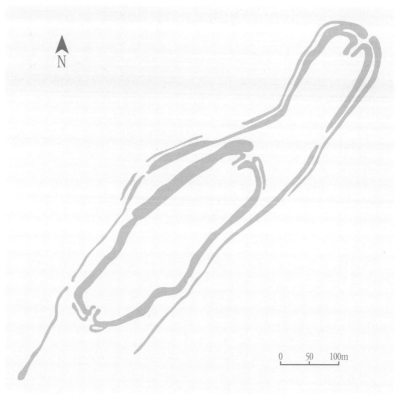

0   50   100m

The Wrekin hillfort

heighten considerably where they form the strong inturned banks of the outer NE entrance (Hell Gate) with its guard room recesses. Only slight remains of the SW outer entrance survive, and its original form is uncertain.

Excavations in 1939 and 1973 have shown that the hilltop was first defended by the outer rampart of simple earth construction. Presumably contemporary with this were a number of 4-post structures, rebuilt many times with dates ranging from the 7th-5th centuries BC. Sometime c.400

BC the inner circuit was built and the outer area abandoned. The inner rampart, initialla dry-stone revetted bank, was later rebuilt and possibly surmounted by a timber palisade. At the same time the inner SW entrance was extended inwards and timber roofed guard rooms added. A possible re-occupation of the outer area in the 2nd century BC may have lasted till the forceful taking of the fort by the Roman army c.49 AD. A Roman javelin head found by the NE gate is graphic evidence for the latter.

Roman and Anglo-Saxon

The arrival of the Roman army in Shropshire sometime in the late 40s AD is represented archaeologically by a series of forts and camps. Of these only the fort at Wall Town near Cleobury Mortimer has surviving earthwork remains. The earliest focal point for this Roman military activity was at Wroxeter, 7km E of Shrewsbury. Following the withdrawal of the army c.90 AD the town of Viriconium Cornoviorum was founded on this now vacated though still strategically important site. It served as the centre for the administration of the territory of the Cornovii, and at its height may have had a population of at least five thousand. As a major urban centre the town was provided with a fine complex of public buildings, the partial remains of which can be seen today.

Unlike many other Roman towns Viriconium survived well beyond the end of Roman administration in Britain. Indeed the town may not have been abandoned until the mid-seventh century, at the time of the assimilation of the region into the expanding Anglo-Saxon Kingdom of Mercia.

The 8th century was the 'Golden Age' of Mercia, and the greatest of all its kings was Offa, who ruled between 757-96. It was he who ordered "the construction of a large rampart the whole way from sea to sea between Britain and Mercia" - what we know today as Offa's Dyke. The Dyke is the longest archaeological monument in Britain, and Shropshire is fortunate in having within its borders some of the finest surviving sections.

This continuous linear earthwork, still standing in places up to 3 metres high and flanked on its west side by a wide ditch, can be seen winding its way across the upland landscapes of west Shropshire. Throughout its entire length the Dyke is sited wherever possible to make use of vantage points overlooking Wales to the west. Intended as a boundary to define the western frontier of Mercia it perhaps also had a symbolic role as a statement of the power and supremacy of Offa and his kingdom.

Less well known is Wat's Dyke, which extends some 61km from the River Morda near Maesbury south of Oswestry to the Dee estuary at Basingwerk. It is essentially the same type of linear earthwork as Offa's Dyke, whose course it runs roughly parallel to in Shropshire, but some 6km to its E. It is usually held to be of the same general date as Offa's frontier, though perhaps pre-dating the latter. Recent excavation of a section of Wat's Dyke near Oswestry has even indicated a possible 5th or 6th century AD date for its construction, which would place it well before the arrival of the Anglo-

Saxons into the area. Regardless of who built it and when, it is likely to have served as a major territorial boundary.

Beyond these linear monuments tangible landscape evidence for the six hundred years following the end of Roman rule in Shropshire is confined to a series of churches containing Anglo-Saxon structural remains. These range from potentially early churches like Wroxeter and Atcham to fine and impressive buildings like Stanton Lacy, perhaps built during the final decades of Anglo-Saxon Shropshire.

28. ACTON BURNELL ROMAN ROAD AND BRIDGE
1st-4th century AD

SJ 525025. 9km S of Shrewsbury. The site is located 600m NW of Acton Burnell. No direct public access, but remains are clearly visible from adjacent public footpath. Path runs N from sharp bend on Acton Burnell-Frodesley road across field for 500m till joining and crossing stream by a footbridge. Monument situated on both banks of stream. Winter visit recommended due to tree cover.

As the great arterial Roman road of Watling Street sweeps SW from Wroxeter it crosses a narrow ravine cut by a stream just to the W of Acton Burnell. The Roman engineers had no option but to cross this obstacle with a bridge, and the surviving remains constitute perhaps the most impressive yet least known legacy of the Roman Empire in Shropshire.

The visually dominant feature is a large embankment that approaches the stream on both sides and which served to carry the road to the crossing point.

The embankment stands up to 4m high and is 6m wide at the top. At the gorge edge it towers some 12m above the stream below. Excavation at the S embankment has shown that only the sandstone footings of the road surface remain, but a substantial stone retaining wall was found along the W side. There are no traces of the presumably wooden bridge that spanned the gorge. This however, was not the earliest road and bridging point. The first road was in the form of a terrace over 10m wide but overlain on its E side by the later embankment. This leads to a bridge, whose S abutment still partially survives. It stands 3.5 m high, is 3m wide, and built of coursed sandstone masonry. Though evidently rebuilt, the abutment is likely to be Roman in origin, and as such is a remarkable survival. The Roman road continues S as a slight hollow-way as it climbs the slope across the field till joining the road to Frodesley. N of the stream and beyond the embankment, Watling Street is marked by a lane that leads NE to Pitchford.

29. WALL TOWN ROMAN FORT
1st-4th century AD

Wall Town Roman Fort - the east rampart

SO 692783. 2.5km NE of Cleobury Mortimer. The fort is bisected by the B4363. No public access, but monument is clearly visible from roadside.

At Wall Town Farm is the only Roman Fort in Shropshire to display visible above ground remains. The surviving earthworks form an almost square enclosure of 2ha with an annexe to the W and formerly to the N. The site is bisected E-W by the B4363 and its N half is built over and obscured by the farm and its outbuildings. The earthworks are best preserved in the pasture field to the S of the road where the rampart stands up to 3m high above a wide outer ditch. It is particularly impressive when seen from the road on the E approach as it rises above steep ground overlooking the Baveney Brook below. The point at

which the road intersects the E rampart marks the probable site of the fort's original E gateway.

Excavations in the 1960s showed the visible fort to be built over an earlier phase of Roman military activity, most likely a larger fort. This was abandoned perhaps in the early 2nd century and replaced by the smaller fort whose surviving rampart was constructed of clay with turf and timber facings. It was fronted by a V-profiled ditch, 3m wide and 2m deep. At a later date a stone wall was inserted in front of the rampart and two further outer ditches added. To the N of the fort a now levelled annexe contained traces of a street and timber buildings, perhaps part of an attached civil 'vicus' settlement.

It seems probable that the second fort was militarily abandoned towards the end of the 2nd century, though some form of later Roman occupation is suggested by 3rd century pottery from the site. The role of the fort must have been to control the difficult upland

area of the Clee Hills. Its continued military occupation well into the 2nd century indicates the importance the military authorities placed on the control of this region.

30. WROXETER ROMAN CITY
1st-4th century AD

SJ 565086. 7km E of Shrewsbury. The B4380 Shrewsbury-Ironbridge road runs adjacent to site. Signposted. EH (*).

The county's best known ancient monument. Indeed, for many Wroxeter is synonymous with Shropshire archaeology. However, claims that Wroxeter is Britain's Pompeii are somewhat exaggerated - this is akin to describing Shrewsbury Town FC as Britain's Real Madrid. Nevertheless, a visit here can be a rewarding experience, providing one does not expect to find streets full of complete buildings, beautifully frescoed villas, and a Neopolitan climate.

A Roman military presence was established at Wroxeter sometime in the late 40s AD and the site remained under military control until the departure of the XX legion c.90 AD. Thereafter the site was developed as the tribal capital of the Cornovii - Viroconium Cornoviorum. By the later 2nd century it had become the fourth largest town in Roman Britain. Only the remains of a small part of the town are visible today, and these are confined to the public baths complex that stood at the heart of its civic centre.

The baths were built between 120-150 AD as a large 'L'-shaped structure with a huge colonnaded exercise hall or basilica on its longer side. Part of the original S wall of the basilica still stands as the tall and impressive piece of masonry known as the Old Work. The large gap through this wall marks the position of the original double-doored entrance that led into the baths suite. The first room entered was the unheated 'frigidarium' that served as a lobby into the heated rooms beyond. It was flanked by two cold plunge baths and roofed with a triple-barrelled vault, whose traces can be seen on the Old Work. Two heavily worn thresholds lead from here into the heated suites. First, two conjoined square rooms, and beyond the larger warm 'tepidarium' room, and then the larger still hot 'caldarium' room. Of these heated rooms only the hypocaust tile pillars that originally supported the floors survive today. In addition there were symmetrically placed subsidiary bath suites on either side of the main rooms, both entered from the unheated room. The W suite was extended in the 3rd century.

On the W side of the baths suites lay an open exercise yard. This contained a shallow open air plunge pool, still visible with its curved ends and paved floor. After some sixty years of use the pool was filled-in - no doubt to the consternation of the Wroxeter Walrus Club. Perhaps they revived their spirits in the town's taverns, two of which may be represented by the two square rooms, each with a central pier base, that abut the SW side of the baths basilica. Conveniently, the town latrine lies behind these two bars. It is a long rectangular room with a deep drain, originally covered by wooden seats, and flushed by water from the baths. The final building in this complex is a most unusual structure - it is a market hall, and comprises a small courtyard, surrounded by small square shops. High quality specialist produce would have been purchased from here, but the town's main market was housed in the forum. Remains of the stone colonnade that fronted the forum can be seen in the field opposite, across the modern road. The forum was completed c.130 AD and a cast of the fine dedicatory inscription that graced the entrance can be seen in the site museum.

All these public buildings are clear evidence of the success and growth of the town during the 2nd century, and the evidence suggests the continuing prosperity of its inhabitants well into the 4th century. Neither does the end of Roman rule in Britain in the early 5th century appear to have had much impact on the town with many of its public buildings remaining in use until the early 6th century. Though by the time of its abandonment sometime in the mid 7th century, it is debatable whether there was truly town life at Wroxeter or merely life in a former town.

Wroxeter Roman City - the public baths complex

31. OFFA'S DYKE, CARREG-Y-BIG - ORSEDDWEN
8th century AD

SJ 252323-251335. 4km NW of Oswestry. From Oswestry take B4580 W for 3.5km, then take road N to Carreg-y-Big. Dyke runs N from roadside opposite Carreg-y-Big Farm. Cross stile, encouragingly marked 'Prestatyn 49 miles' and follow path alongside Dyke for 1.2km as far as county boundary just S of Orseddwen.

There are few finer stretches of Offa's Dyke than that which runs N from Carreg-y-Big. As it ascends the rising ground it is built on a massive scale. The steeply scarped bank, surmounted by a modern field wall, towers some 5m high above the wide, deep ditch. Despite increasing scrub growth on the earthwork, it presents an impressive spectacle. On reaching the level hill summit the Dyke enters a fine stand of beech trees and here for a length of c.120m it is almost perfect. Beyond this a spring rises in a gap through the Dyke, and thereafter the earthwork crosses the plateau in a straight alignment. Along this level section, though still finely preserved, the bank is less massive and the ditch is partially waterlogged due to doubling up here as a drainage channel. The earthwork then descends to cross a stream, from which point onwards it forms the boundary between England and Wales for the next three miles. The Dyke can be seen climbing the hillside to the N, but there is no public access to it beyond Orseddwen Farm.

Offa's Dyke north of Carreg-y-Big

32. OFFA'S DYKE, DUDSTON
8th century AD

SO 253974 - 236971.
12km NW of Bishop's Castle.
From Chirbury take the B4386
W for 2.5km. Offa's Dyke is
visible extending S from the
road. Access to monument
via stile from roadside and
footpath along Dyke.

This section of Offa's Dyke is somewhat unusual in that it crosses generally low-lying ground and does not command the extensive westward views that are so characteristic of the monument's siting elsewhere along its course.

Immediately S of the B4386 the Dyke survives for a length of c.160m as a well preserved earthwork up to 3m high and with a ditch over 2m deep.

A short distance along this section is a narrow gap through the earthwork which marks the original crossing point of the Chirbury-Montgomery road prior to the present turnpike road being put through in 1768. Either side of the Dyke can be seen ridge and furrow, which, despite appearances to the contrary, is not cut through by the Dyke. For the next 200m or so there is little or no trace of the W ditch but the bank remains impressive. At first some 1.6m high it heightens considerably into an enormous sharp profiled bank. Beyond this point the county and national boundary follows the line of the Dyke for the next 3km, straight as an arrow in a NW-SE direction. The earthwork itself survives intermittently along this length.

33. OFFA'S DYKE, SPOAD HILL - LLANFAIR HILL
8th century AD

SO 254808-256784. 4.5km W
of Clun. From Clun take B4368
W for 5km. At Middle Spoad
follow minor road S for 1.5km
up steep hill to crossroads at
Spoad Hill. Road S runs parallel
to Offa's Dyke for c.1km. Dyke
visible from road and thereafter
visible from trackway that forks
SE from road and parallel to W
side of Dyke for further 1.5km.

Perhaps the most magnificent section of all along the entire length of Offa's Dyke. Not only does its scale impress here but also its scenic impact as it

snakes across the upland splendour of the Clun Forest hills. From Springhill Farm a fine straight section heads S parallel to the road, before descending a small valley where it is crossed by a stream through a narrow gap. It then sweeps majestically up the opposing valley slope as it climbs to the Llanfair Hill plateau. The earthwork is at its most massive here - a broad tall bank, deep wide ditch, and also a low counterscarp along the W tip of the ditch. A further broad shallow and irregularly edged probable quarry ditch flanks the E side of the bank.

On reaching the level hill summit the dyke, though less substantial, is still a commanding structure. Llanfair Hill at 408m is the highest point reached by the Dyke in the whole of its course

'from sea to sea'. Nowhere is the power and grandeur of 8th century Mercia better displayed than here on this windswept south Shropshire height.

Offa's Dyke as it climbs up to Llanfair Hill

34. WAT'S DYKE, OSWESTRY
5th-8th century AD

SJ 297293. On E side of Oswestry town. Best approached from S side of Middleton Road where a footpath leads S and alongside W side of Wat's Dyke.

Though now hemmed in on all sides by housing development this section of Wat's Dyke is still worth a visit. It runs straight N-S for a length of some 350m. The bank is well preserved and is a prominent

feature averaging c.1.5m high, though higher at its S end. Its top carries a line of fine mature trees. Virtually all trace of the W flanking ditch has disappeared here, but this would have been an equally impressive feature. Excavations have shown the ditch to have averaged 4m deep and over 5m wide, which when coupled with the originally 3m high bank would have made the whole Dyke system some 15m wide.

35. WAT'S DYKE, PREESHENLLE
5th-8th century AD

Wat's Dyke north of Preeshenlle

SJ 308359-306348. 5km N of Oswestry. From roundabout in Gobowen take B5069 N for 800m. Then take turning to left, signposted Henlle. Follow the road N till reaching road junction. Footpath on N side of road junction runs alongside Wat's Dyke.

This is a good section of the Dyke that runs for a length of some 500m. It heads downhill through a belt of woodland and here the bank stands in places up to 2m high, though the W ditch has been largely filled in. After c.350m the line of the Dyke crosses the Shropshire Union Canal by a bridge. As the Dyke approaches the bridge from both sides the canal engineers have cleverly used its bank to form the approach ramps of the bridge. Beyond the canal the Dyke continues to descend as a wide grassy bank, crossing a marshy area before rising up the other side till disappearing beneath a disused railway embankment.

Retrace your steps to the crossroads then follow the road S for 500m. Immediately S of Walnut Lodge and running alongside the rhs of the road is a fine 100m length of the Dyke. Though somewhat masked by tree cover its characteristic form can clearly be seen. The ditch still survives impressively here, partially waterlogged by a watercourse that runs along it.

36. ST EATA'S CHURCH, ATCHAM
8th-9th century AD

SJ 541092. 5km SE of Shrewsbury. On S side of B4380, immediately SE of bridge across River Severn.

A chocolate box setting on the banks of the Severn for this gem of a church. It was here in 1075 that the Anglo-Norman historian Ordericus Vitalis was baptised as a child. The nave of that church still stands today. Its tall thick side walls lean alarmingly outwards - hence the huge external buttresses, dated 1817. Both N and S walls are built of large squared stones - reused stones from Roman Wroxeter, just 2km distant. The N wall stands on a square-sectioned stone plinth that turns S at the NW angle. Its W quoins are formed of massive stones well laid in side alternate fashion.

High up at the E end of the N wall is a small single splayed window. Externally it is round-headed, but internally it has a triangular head formed of two angular laid slabs running through the thickness of the wall - a characteristic Anglo-Saxon constructional technique. The general absence of late-Saxon features in the pre-conquest fabric has led to suggestions

A wall in St Eata's Church, Atcham

that the nave may be as early as 8th century in date.

Also of interest is the unique church dedication to St Eata, the 7th century Northumbrian Bishop of Hexham and Lindisfarne. Could this be due to a personal association of the saint with Atcham? After all, the place-name enshrines the name 'Eata'. Or, did the dedication arise from the place-name? Intriguing.

37. ST GILES CHURCH, BARROW
10th-11th century AD

SO 658999. 3 km E of Much Wenlock. Set back from S side of B4376 Much Wenlock - Broseley road adjacent to Hall and farm buildings.

Barrow was part of the large Anglo-Saxon Minster parish of Much Wenlock. By the mid 11th century the Minster had built a chapel here. Of this chapel the chancel certainly, and nave possibly, of the present church survive

Barrow Church - Anglo-Saxon chancel arch

largely intact. The tiny chancel, just 6m x 4m internally is of late 10th or 11th century date. Its walls of large, dressed and coursed masonry stand on a tall triple-stepped plinth, similar to that at Diddlebury. A single pilaster strip extends from the top of the plinth in the middle of the N wall. High in the E end of the N wall is an original double-splayed window, this too similar to that at Diddlebury. Most impressive of all is the chancel arch - the only surviving Anglo-Saxon example in Shropshire. It has a square-sectioned hood moulding on its W face, and originally square imposts that were "most foolishly chamfered" in 1851. The chancel E wall was rebuilt in the 19th century.

The rubble built nave could be either Norman or pre-conquest. It is aisle-less, with three original tall single-splayed windows and tall simple narrow doorways in the N, S and W walls. The larger W doorway, now the tower arch, with its diaper-patterned tympanum, was the original main entrance prior to the erection of the 12th century W tower.

Evidence from an earlier, narrower, and possibly wooden nave is visible on the internal E wall of the nave, where the masonry of the chancel W wall and gable stands out boldly against the later nave walling.

38. ST PETER'S CHURCH, DIDDLEBURY
10th-11th century AD

SO 508853. 8km NE of Craven Arms. On E side of Diddlebury village 600m E of B4368 Craven Arms-Bridgnorth road.

Of this fine church the N wall of the nave, and part of the adjoining N wall of the tower are Anglo-Saxon work of exceptionally high quality. Externally the nave N wall is built on a tall plinth of three square orders which can be seen to turn S at the E end, marking the original NE angle of the pre-conquest nave. Above the plinth the Anglo-Saxon fabric rises to a height of 4.5m and is built of large well dressed stone blocks. At the W end of the wall is an original round-headed doorway,

now blocked, of typical tall narrow proportions. It is externally framed by projecting strip work of square section, while its sill is formed by the lowest course of the wall plinth. High up in the wall toward the E end is an impressive double-splayed window - a diagnostically Anglo-Saxon feature. Its narrow mid-wall aperture is set in a stone slab that carries an external rebate for the probable housing of a wooden shutter.

Internally the wall face is of completely different character, having a superbly impressive herring-bone facing of specially cut stones that is clearly contemporary with the rest of the pre-conquest fabric. It fulfils no structural function here and must be purely a decorative treatment. Note the two Anglo-Saxon carved stone panels set into and below the internal faces of windows in the nave N wall. One with simple interlace, the other probably depicting a Tree of Jesse.

This Anglo-Saxon church must have had a W annexe or tower as evidenced by the continuation of the nave wall plinth beneath the E part of the tower N wall. Also by the similarity of this section of the tower fabric to that of the nave N wall. All the pre-conquest structural remains are consistent with a probable early 11th century date for what must have been an important and impressive late Saxon church.

St Peter's Church, Diddlebury

St Peter's Church, Stanton Lacy - nave west wall

39. ST PETER'S CHURCH, STANTON LACY
11th century AD

SO 495788. 4km N of Ludlow.

The finest of all the county's Anglo-Saxon churches. Try visiting at snowdrop time when the churchyard is a dazzling blanket of white. It is a large and ambitious 11th century cruciform church, of which the nave N and W walls and N transept survive largely complete. The Anglo-Saxon walls are decorated with narrow projecting pilaster strips of long and short construction which rise from square blocks. Unlike those on the N transept the nave pilasters do not extend almost the full height of the walls, suggesting the upper walls have been rebuilt. Those strips on the N transept have short cross pieces. In the nave N wall is an exceptionally fine original doorway. Tall, narrow and round-headed, it is flanked by pilaster strips and its head framed by a chamfered hood moulding. A simple carved cross is set above the doorway,

and above this rises a pilaster strip resting on a short cross-piece surmounting a row of four carved balls. Internally, on the N wall of the transept are the partial remains of the head of a blocked pre-conquest doorway, its position is marked externally by an area of irregular masonry.

Legend tells how St Milburga (Abbess at Wenlock from 675-727) founded the church at Stanton Lacy in gratitude to God for successfully defending her virginity here on the banks of the River Corve. Fanciful perhaps - but consider this: The church sits within a large, originally circular churchyard, of which only the S half now survives, and bounded by a raised bank. Could this perhaps represent a former monastic enclosure? Archaeology and folklore combining here to hint at an early monastic origin for the church site at Stanton Lacy.

40. ST ANDREW'S CHURCH, WROXETER
8th-9th century AD

SJ 563082. 7km SE of Shrewsbury. In centre of Wroxeter village, 600m S of B4380 Shrewsbury-Ironbridge Road.

The pair of Roman columns either side of the churchyard gate will immediately whet the appetite of any visitor to this archaeologically important church. Those in search of antiquity should make straight for the N side of the

church. The E 12m of the nave N wall is what survives of the original N wall of an Anglo-Saxon nave. It is conspicuously built of large squared stones, all re-used Roman material, and stands on a square plinth first revealed by excavation in 1985. The W end of this early nave with its massive side alternate quoining is clearly visible as a straight joint abutting the later medieval extension.

St Andrew's Church, Wroxeter - Anglo-Saxon carved panel in S wall of nave

An original pre-conquest small square window, now blocked, sits high in the centre of the wall. The wall carries a projecting square string course along its top. A date as early as the 8th century has been suggested for this Anglo-Saxon building, which itself was perhaps built on the site of a British monastic predecessor.

The S nave wall was rebuilt in 1763, and set in it high up is a piece of cross shaft, flanked by two stone panels, each carved with an animal. These are part of an Anglo-Saxon cross shaft that stood in the churchyard until the 18th century. Another carved stone depicting birds pecking at snakes is built into the S base of the chancel arch. All are fine pieces of Mercian work of 8th or early 9th century date. Together, these remains are graphic evidence of the Anglo-Saxon Christian community that once flourished at Wroxeter.

Castles

The arrival of the Normans in Shropshire after 1066 brought with it that most familiar of all monuments of the Middle Ages - the castle. The large number of castles in Shropshire illustrates the Normans' determination to stamp their control and authority over this strategically important border region. The castles of the later 11th century were largely constructed of earth and timber and were mainly of the 'motte and bailey' type. These comprised the motte, a circular conical mound of earth, originally surmounted by a tall timber tower at its centre, and with a defensive palisade around its perimeter. Adjoined to the motte were one or more baileys, enclosures defended usually by a palisaded bank and ditch. These would have housed all the essential ancillary buildings such as stores, stabling and accommodation for the garrison.

Another type of early Norman castle was the ringwork. These are enclosures, usually but not always circular in shape, defended by a bank and ditch, and often with a strong gatehouse tower, but no motte. These too would have been provided with baileys as at the Marche Hall ringwork.

From the 12th century onwards many castles were refurbished in stone. Timber palisades were replaced by masonry curtain walls, and lofty tower keeps, such as at Bridgnorth and Ludlow, constructed in place of the wooden motte towers. The tower keep is perhaps the most enduring and visually spectacular element of medieval castle architecture. In their hey-day these great towers were very much a psychological symbol of lordship and it may be this that explains why they continued to be built in Shropshire into the 14th century.

Advances in castle design were, however, readily employed in Shropshire castles. During the 13th century in particular there was a move towards adopting a more offensive as opposed to defensive role for castles. This involved placing greater emphasis on the curtain wall with projecting mural towers and increasingly elaborate and strong gatehouses. Whittington Castle is a fine example of this new design trend.

Following the conquest and pacification of Wales in the late 13th century many castles lost their primary military function. Those that remained in use often show evidence of an increased emphasis on domestic provision. Nowhere is this better seen than at Clun with its large and lavish 'residential' tower of c.1300.

By the end of the Middle Ages most Shropshire castles had probably been abandoned, and those that remained were in a poor state of repair. They were, however, to have one final fling of glory during the Civil War in the 1640s.

Even after centuries of decay and neglect castles like Shrewsbury, Ludlow and Bridgnorth were defiantly to withstand sieges for many months before eventually surrendering to an end made inevitable by gunpowder.

41. ACTON BURNELL CASTLE
13th century AD

SJ 534019. 12km SE of Shrewsbury. From crossroads in centre of Acton Burnell take road E for 200m, then turn right. Entry to castle is 200m up lane on lhs. EH

This fortified manor house, for castle it is not, is a testimony to the prestige and ambition of one man - Robert Burnell. Friend of Edward 1, Bishop of Bath and Wells, and Lord Chancellor, Burnell was "next to the King himself, the chief figure in the political life of

the realm" until his death in 1292. In 1284 the King granted him "licence for the construction of his manor at Acton Burnell". The result is the splendid ruin seen today.

The manor house is all of one date and consists of a rectangular structure with projecting square towers of four stages at the corners and a projecting garderobe block at the W end. The main central block contained a great hall at first floor level, divided centrally by an arcade, and lit by large traceried

Acton Burnell Castle

windows. Its main approach was probably up an external stair through the NE tower which also served as a porch. This same tower housed a chapel at first floor level. A great chamber lay beyond the hall at the W end. Above this was a single room containing Burnell's private apartment and accessed via a spiral stair in the SW tower. The ground floor is likely to have accommodated the Bishop's household and officials and comprised office, chamber and a small hall. The two large arches in the ground floor N and S walls were inserted in the 18th century when the building was used as a barn.

The surviving structure must have formed the main dwelling only of a more extensive manorial complex. Part of this can be seen 90m to the E where stand the gable ends of an extremely long medieval aisled barn. Tradition has this barn as the venue for the historic Parliament of 1283 held at Acton Burnell - nice story but unlikely.

42. BRIDGNORTH CASTLE
12th century AD

SO 717927. On S side of town centre, inside Town Park close to its N entrance.

Of this once large and important royal castle only the ruinous keep survives - but what a ruin it is. It towers over the jutting promontory that formerly held the castle inner bailey, now the Town Park. Founded in 1101 by Robert de Belleme to replace his father's castle at Quatford 3 km to the SE, it was taken the following year by Henry I after a three month siege. Thereafter it remained in royal hands for the next five centuries.

Between 1155-89 £300 was spent on the castle, and some at least, of this will have been lavished on the building of the keep. Its spectacular and somewhat alarming leaning appearance, 15° from the vertical, is the result of being blown up by Parliamentary forces in 1646 following a successful siege. Originally it stood over 21m high, was some 10m square, and its walls, up to 3m thick at the base, were clasped with flat buttresses at the angles. The masonry of its upper part is well-cut ashlar of grey sandstone, the lower part of a soft red sandstone. Putlog holes for carrying scaffolding are evident on the outer face of the N wall. The tower held three storeys and was no doubt entered at first floor level. There are remains of a fireplace in the S wall of the first floor, and remains of a double-splayed window in the W wall on the second. High up on the inside N wall can be seen the projecting moulding of the inverted roofline. Remnants of a probable fore-building abut on to the W side of the tower, and a large fragment of masonry to the SE is likely to be the topmost portion of the keep's SE angle.

Nearby, the church of St Mary Magdalene, rebuilt 1792, stands on the site of the castle chapel in the former inner bailey. The larger outer bailey extended N and is today partly fossilised by the line of East and West Castle Streets.

Bridgnorth Castle - the Keep

43. CASTLE PULVERBATCH
11th-12th century AD

SJ 422022. 12km SW of Shrewsbury. The castle stands on the S edge of Pulverbatch village and is readily accessible from the adjacent road.

A terrific earthwork, this Norman stronghold is a powerful statement of medieval

lordship, well befitting the caput of the 12th century Barony of Pulverbatch. Built high on a promontory of great natural strength, it overlooks and commands an ancient valley route along which passed the main medieval road from Shrewsbury to Bishop's Castle. The tall conical motte, partially quarried on its W side, rises over 8m high above the broad and deep ditch surrounding its base. The smaller of two conjoined baileys abuts the NE side of the motte. It is roughly rectangular in shape and is defended on its N and E by a stout rampart 10m wide and over 4m high above an outer ditch. On its SE side where the natural hill-slope is precipitous there is no bank or ditch, only a scarp. A large hollow on the bailey edge immediately adjacent to the motte could mark the site of an abutment for the bridge that would have originally connected motte with bailey. The larger triangular shaped outer bailey lies to the NW of the motte, and like its counterpart is protected by a bank and ditch though of less substantial size. Two low rectangular platforms in its W sector probably mark the site of former buildings.

The village of Pulverbatch, a short distance N of the castle, has a distinctly regular plan, perhaps suggestive of its origin as a deliberate foundation by the lord of the manor in the 12th or 13th century. The castle itself, though probably erected in the later 11th century, is first mentioned in 1153. It was still occupied in 1205 but there was said to be no manor house here in 1292.

Castle Pulverbatch

44. CLUN CASTLE
11th-14th century AD

SO 299809. Situated on the W edge of Clun. Best approached from public car park adjacent to Clun Bridge. From here cross river via timber footbridge and follow path to castle. EH

A wonderful monument, its gaunt ruins stand sentinel-like above the valley and town of Clun. Though first mentioned in 1140, the castle was probably founded by Picot de Say who held the manor in

1086. A natural spur of land in a bend of the River Clun was scarped and enhanced to form a massive oval motte divided by a deep ditch from two separate raised baileys. The S bailey was entered via a causeway from the S side of the motte. It is defended by a ditch and an inner rampart on all but the W side, where runs the river and the steepest slopes. A further causeway connects with the smaller bailey to the E, now used as a bowling green.

The castle passed by marriage to the FitzAlans c.1150, who from 1243 became the Earls of Arundel. Until 1549 they held the castle as the caput of the Barony of Clun. It was the FitzAlans who were responsible for building the most spectacular of the surviving castle buildings - the Great Tower built into the N side of the motte. Four-storeyed and 28m high it has all the appearance of a Norman keep - but it is not. It dates to the late 13th century and comprises suites of separate lodgings, possibly serving as up-market accommodation for the high status guests of the Earls of Arundel. Edward I visited in 1295 and Edward III stayed at Clun to hunt in 1362. The tower was meant to impress both visually and psychologically. As a physical expression of the power and prestige of one of the great baronial families of medieval England it was perhaps consciously built to resemble a tower keep - that traditional symbol of dominion.

The motte summit was surrounded by a curtain wall, of which a section survives between two projecting solid half-round towers on the S perimeter. The footprint of a probable twin-towered gatehouse is discernible at the E end overlooking the bailey causeway.

From the motte, looking across to the W bank of the River Clun, can be seen a square complex of now dry moats and fishponds. These mark the site of a medieval 'pleasance' or pleasure garden. This unusual and rare survival emphasises the fact that Clun, like all castles, was at once both a military stronghold and a private residence.

45. ELLESMERE CASTLE
11th century AD

SJ 403347. On E edge of Ellesmere. Footpath, signposted Castle Mound, leads directly from Shrewsbury Road (opposite Meres Visitor Centre) to castle earthworks.

It is likely to have been Roger de Montgomery, Earl of Shrewsbury, who founded the castle at Ellesmere sometime after c.1070. The site chosen was the summit of a conspicuous ridge commanding splendid views in all directions and particularly to the N over the great lake called The Mere. The castle comprises a huge motte with a disproportionately small bailey. The tree clad steep-sided motte has a base diameter of 80m and rises 11m to its broad flat summit which is used as a bowling green. A wide and deep ditch separates the mound from its bailey on the E side. The bailey takes the form of a crescent shaped platform defended by a ditch of

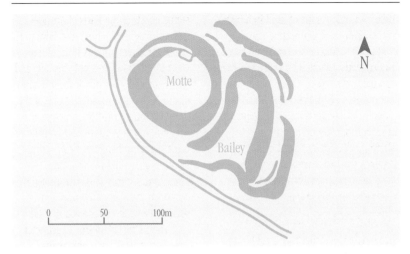

Ellesmere Castle

massive proportions, particularly on the E side where it is cut into a steep natural slope, and here with a substantial outer bank. This bailey is narrow, only 20-30m wide, though it would originally have extended further S, before being truncated by the existing road and further eroded by partial quarrying. The relatively small size of the bailey is probably explained by a much larger principal bailey having

formerly extended to the W of the motte along the projecting ridge top. This area is occupied by the 19th century rectory and its grounds.

A series of substantial terraces and scarps in the grounds, although probably 19th century in their present form, may well be a remodelling of earlier bailey defences.

46. HOCKLETON MOTTE AND BAILEY
11th-12th century AD

SO 274999. 12km N of Bishop's Castle. Access is via public footpath leading E from B4386 to Hockleton Farm. Go through farmyard and follow path which leads to site in the field immediately S of farm.

A small but interesting little motte and bailey at the end of a ridge and overlooking a narrow gorge to its E. The well preserved circular motte, ditched only on its E side, stands 4m high

with a tiny top just 6m in diameter. Only the smallest of structures could have stood on its summit. The motte sits within and forms the S side of a roughly crescent-shaped bailey that survives as a raised, but ditchless platform.

A 6m wide gap through the bailey scarp on its N side represents the original entrance. A later hollow-way runs through the entrance and across the bailey. Another hollow-way runs immediately to the SW, and there are slight traces of ridge and furrow to the N and S of the castle earthworks. This castle is but one of a number of small timber castles in the Vale of Montgomery, which, because of their similarity, have been suggested as resulting from a late 11th century colonisation of the area by the tenants of Roger of Montgomery.

47. HOPTON CASTLE
12th-14th century AD

SO 366779. 9km SW of Craven Arms. Take B4367 to Hopton Heath. From here take road W to Hopton Castle. Castle lies on S side of road through village. No public access but monument clearly visible from roadside.

The great tower keep that so dominates this monument appears at first sight to be a typical Norman keep, but closer inspection reveals it to have been built in the early 14th century. As such it is one of a number of tower keeps of late 13th/ early 14th century date in Shropshire. This display of conscious anachronism by the nobility shows the conservative nature of medieval Shropshire - no change there then.

The keep is an impressive sight, its tall rectangular outline framed against the backdrop of the Shropshire Hills. Square in plan and three-storeyed, it has buttress-like corner turrets, that on the NE angle containing a spiral staircase. There are ground floor doors on the N and W sides, with remains of a causeway leading from the base of the W door.

The tower stands on a low circular motte surrounded by a wide and partially water-

Hopton Castle

filled ditch. Indeed water would clearly have played an important role in the defence of the castle, sited as it is in a valley bottom location at the confluence of two streams. A rectangular inner bailey lies immediately to the W of the motte. Spreads of stone along its edges suggest a former curtain wall, and a square hollow at its SW corner, a probable tower. Well preserved building platforms occupy its NE quadrant. A second outer bailey lies to the S and W in the form of a large L-shaped platform encompassed on all but its W side by a wide originally water-

filled ditch. This ditch widens out at the NE to create a rectangular fishpond.

In March 1644 the castle was the scene of one of the most brutal acts of the Civil War. After a bloody two week siege the small Parliamentarian garrison surrendered. The siege had cost the lives of over two hundred Royalist soldiers. In revenge all twenty-eight of the vanquished were stripped, kept naked on the cold winter's day for an hour and then clubbed to death. Think on that while you enjoy the tranquil scene today.

48. LITTLE NESS MOTTE AND BAILEY
11th-12th century AD

Little Ness motte and bailey

SJ 408198. 22km NW of Shrewsbury. On N side of Little Ness village, alongside minor road that leads N from village war memorial towards the church.

This nice little earthwork castle site occupies the top of a low hill overlooking Little Ness village to its S. The motte stands at the end of the S spur of the hillock. It is 5m high, roughly oval in shape, with a summit of c.4m radius. Part of its S side has been dug away, making it somewhat D-shaped. This may be the result of a 19th century excavation which apparently encountered "animal bones and burnt wood".

Immediately, to the NW lies the small, charming 12th century church of St Martin. It sits within an oval churchyard whose elevated position is further enhanced by its artificially scarped perimeter enclosed by a retaining wall. This churchyard is likely to be the original castle bailey. It is physically separated from the motte by a ditch which does not, however, extend around the remainder of the motte base. A second bailey may also have lain to the S of the motte, represented today by an area of level ground defined along its S by a scarp. Note how the present road skirts around this area suggesting a former landscape feature of some antiquity.

49. LUDLOW CASTLE
11th-17th century AD

SO 508746. In centre of Ludlow at W end of Castle Square. (*)

If you like your castles big, a bit flashy, and topped off with a dollop of historical romance, then this is one for you. If not, go and give it a try, you might still enjoy it. Ludlow Castle was probably begun by Walter de Lacy sometime before 1085, and is unusual in having been stone built from the outset. Over the next 500 years the castle was to develop into one of the great fortresses of the Marches.

The early Norman castle consisted of a walled enclosure fronted to S and E by a rock-cut ditch. This now forms the inner bailey. Entry was originally through a large gatehouse tower on its S side, heightened in the later 12th century to form the sturdy tower keep that so dominates today. The original gateway arch, now blocked, is still visible on the lower outer face of the keep. The defences were completed by a series of rectangular towers projecting from the tall curtain wall. It was beneath these walls that King Stephen gallantly rescued Prince Henry of Scotland from the clutches of a grappling hook during a siege of the castle in 1139.

The most remarkable of the Norman buildings in the inner bailey is the chapel of St Mary Magdalene. It is unusual in having a circular nave, and a fine one it is too, with its ornamental doorways and internal wall arcading. It dates to c.1140. Late in the 12th century the castle was quadrupled in size by the addition of a large rectangular outer bailey to the S and E. Its main gate, still the main entry today, was on the E side, while on the W side a second gatehouse was later incorporated into the semi-circular Mortimer's Tower. A new entry was also inserted through the curtain wall of the now inner bailey replacing that formerly through the gatehouse tower.

Ludlow Castle - the inner bailey

The 1280s saw the start of the next major building programme within the inner bailey. To this era belongs the splendid Great Hall together with a two-storey solar block at its W end. It was completed in the 1320s by the construction of the Great Chamber Block to the E of the hall and an attached projecting garderobe tower. This latter tower is said to be haunted, and sounds of heavy breathing have been claimed to emanate from it - though causes other than the supernatural also spring to mind. For a short time during the 1320s these fine buildings served almost as the private palace of the great Roger Mortimer, first Earl of March and paramour of Queen Isabella. He it was also who built the chapel of St Peter in the SW angle of the outer bailey.

Unlike most Shropshire castles Ludlow continued to be a place of great importance in the post-medieval period. This was because it became the headquarters of the Council in the Marches of Wales between 1501-1689. Its role as administrative capital of Wales and the Marches is architecturally reflected in a range of 16th century buildings. These include the Porter's Lodge, prison and stables on the E side of the outer bailey, and the Judges Lodgings in the inner bailey.

50. MARCHE HALL RINGWORK
11th-12th century AD

SJ 342108. 14km W of Shrewsbury. From Halfway House take B4387 S for 600m, park on lhs of road just before railway crossing. Continue across railway line and along road for c.150m, then cross stile on rhs of road (opposite

Marche Hall ringwork

Stonedale Cottage) and follow path SW along hedge for 300m. Cross stile and follow path N alongside hedge for 200m till reaching monument.

From a distance this ringwork castle stands tantalisingly silhouetted against the skyline. It is prominently situated on the summit of a round hillock at the end of a low ridge and seemingly in the middle of nowhere. The earthwork is a roughly oval enclosure comprising a flat topped platform with scarped sides standing some 1.6m above the surrounding land. Possible building platforms are evident on the N and E

sectors of the interior. The defensive ditch that would have originally encircled the ringwork now survives only as a shallow depression on the SW side. Ploughing has also largely obliterated traces of the elongated bailey that was attached to and extended from the N side of the ringwork.

The present day isolated siting of this castle is a little misleading, for there is nearby field name evidence to suggest that it lay in or close to the now vanished hamlet of Brerelawe, first recorded in the 13th century but whose date of desertion has not been established.

51. MORE MOTTE AND BAILEY
11th-12th century AD

SO 339914. 3km NE of Bishops Castle. From the A488 road 1km NW of Lydham take the minor road E to More. Castle lies in field on W edge

of village and is crossed by public footpath leading W from road as it turns into village.

In the time of Henry I (1100-35) the Lord of More was required to command

200 foot soldiers whenever the King crossed into Wales in time of war. He was to march in the vanguard of the army and personally carry the King's standard. Today the castle earthworks at More stand as a reminder of this feudal lord's power base.

A seemingly typical motte and bailey stands amidst low-lying meadows formerly surrounded by marsh, hence the place-name, More - marsh. In fact excavation has shown that the low flat topped motte began life as a ringwork which was later filled in and heightened to form the present mound. It is surrounded by a wide partially water-filled ditch, with an outer bank. To the E is a square shaped inner bailey containing well preserved building platforms and internal sub-divisions. A possible fishpond abuts its

N side. Beyond lies a larger outer bailey partially defended by a bank and ditch and with a broad hollow-way running through it. This hollow-way connects the points of entry into both baileys. The entrance on the E side of the outer bailey is flanked by the earthworks of a probable gatehouse that overlooks a causeway across the defensive ditch. From the causeway the hollow-way continues to curve N to join the present road into More village. A length of bank E of the hollow-way alongside the present road has been claimed to be part of a third outer bailey which may have contained the original village of More. However, it seems equally likely that the village has always occupied its present position, centred on the 12th century church of St Peter, 200m E of the castle.

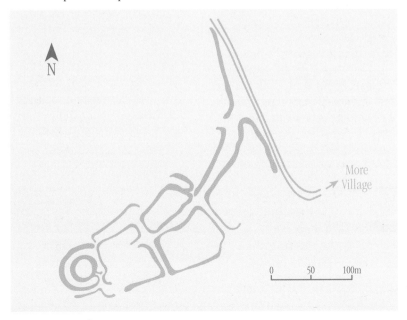

More motte and bailey

52. MORETON CORBET CASTLE
12th-17th century AD

Moreton Corbet Castle

SJ 561232. 7km SE of Wem. From Shawbury take the B5063 N for 1.5km. Castle is signposted to E and lies 250m at end of minor road. EH

A magnificently romantic ruin that creates a memorable silhouette against the North Shropshire skyline. It is dominated by the huge Elizabethan south range with its visually spectacular south facade, see the date 1579 at the SE corner. The inspiration for this was Robert Corbet, courtier and diplomat. After his death in 1583 the house was left unfinished. Corbet family heraldry still embellishes the facade - look out for cute little squirrels, malevolent ravens, and rustic elephants.

The building of this and the slightly earlier, though more ruinous E range extended out beyond the S side of the earlier medieval castle. This castle was probably established in the 12th century by the Toret family, and acquired through marriage by the Corbets c.1239.

It comprised a roughly triangular enclosure with a keep on its W edge and a gatehouse at the N apex. The small rectangular keep dates to c.1200 and only its N and parts of the E and W walls survive. It is of three levels, with a large hooded fireplace in the first floor chamber. The heavily rebuilt medieval curtain wall extends in straight sections from keep to gatehouse. It can be seen to abut and therefore post-date the keep, and presumably replaced an earlier timber palisade. Although the gatehouse was heightened and remodelled in 1579, its core is basically medieval, perhaps of the 14th century. A ditch which formerly surrounded the whole of the castle can still be traced along the E and W sides.

During the Civil War the castle was considered sufficiently strong to be garrisoned by a force of 110 Royalists. This did not prevent it being taken by a mere ten Parliamentarian troops in 1644. It had ceased to be the residence of the Corbets by the 18th century.

53. OSWESTRY CASTLE
11th-12th century AD

SJ 290298. In the centre of Oswestry, between Bailey Head and Horsemarket.

This once strategically important castle is represented today by a large and lofty oval mound, perhaps mainly of natural origin, that formed the castle motte. It is c.12m high, and on the N and E sides of the flat summit are the collapsed remains of a stone keep with walls 2.5m thick. This probably rectangular keep must have been a substantial structure, for an inventory of 1398 refers to it as containing three chambers, a hall, wardrobe, and chapel. A reconstructed probable bastion projects from the E edge of the motte top.

In 1897-99 the mound was landscaped to create a series of terraced paths around its slopes. Revetment walls were also built, possibly incorporating re-used medieval masonry. Abutting the revetment wall at the SW base of the mount is a short section of the 13th century town wall, which here crossed the motte ditch to join the body of the castle mound. The wall is 2m wide with a rubble core, and a facing of dressed stone blocks. The castle bailey, of which nothing now survives above ground, extended S of the motte, and its general location is today indicated by the street names Bailey Head and Bailey Street.

Oswestry Castle - the motte

The castle is first mentioned in 1086 when it is referred to simply as 'Luvre' or 'The Work', then newly built by Rainald, Sheriff of Shropshire. In the early 12th century it passed to the FitzAlan's who held it throughout the Middle Ages. It was besieged in 1644 and thereafter slighted and dismantled by order of Parliament.

54. QUATFORD MOTTE AND BAILEY
11th century AD

SO 7389007. 2.5km SE of Bridgnorth. From car parking area S of Quatford church cross A442 and follow footpath leading N alongside fence parallel to road. On reaching stile cross into field; path continues W alongside wall and across S side of monument.

Shortly before 1086 Roger de Montgomery, Earl of Shrewsbury, founded here at Quatford a collegiate church, a borough, and a 'New House'. The church still stands; of the borough there are no remains. As for the 'New House' its site today is probably represented by the earthworks of a little known but fine motte and bailey castle in a truly spectacular location. It sits perched on a sheer sandstone cliff top high above the E bank of the river Severn.

The castle is carved out of a broad ridge with the motte at its W end. The motte is separated from the bailey by a 2.5m deep rock cut ditch from the base of which the mound rises 10m to the summit. To anyone approaching from the N and W 900 years ago, it must have looked formidable and intimidating, surmounted by its tall timber tower and stockade. The ditchless bailey spans the natural ridge as a platform with scarped sides on its N and S. Its E edge is truncated by the cutting of the A442 road. Prior to the widening of the road in 1960

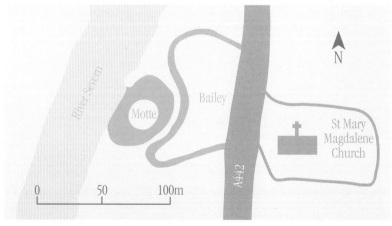

Quatford motte and bailey

excavation revealed a complex of postholes, but little else, and no dating evidence. The churchyard and church of St Mary Magdalene, with its Norman nave and chancel, overlooks the castle from the E.

Perhaps it was this potential topographical weakness that prompted Robert de Belleme to abandon Quatford in 1101 and move the whole complex - castle, college and borough - 3km upstream to Bridgnorth.

55. SHRAWARDINE CASTLE
11th-13th century AD

SJ 400154. 9km W of Shrewsbury. Shrawardine is signposted off the A5 (T) road. The Castle lies in field opposite Shrawardine church and is accessed via public footpath leading from roadside kissing gate.

Built to control the nearby ford across the Severn, Shrawardine Castle was first recorded in 1165. John FitzAlan of Oswestry had possession by 1240 and he renamed it Castle Isabel in honour of his wife. The castle remained in

FitzAlan ownership till 1583. During the Civil War it was a staunch Royalist base under the command of Sir William Vaughan, the 'Devil of Shrawardine'. His brother Charles however, was of less stern stuff; and he it was who 'cowardlye surrendered' the castle after just three days siege in 1645. Thereafter the castle was demolished and its stonework "carried to Shrewsbury for the repayring of the castle there".

It is the motte that visually dominates the site today. Oblong in shape, it stands up to 4m high. On its W side

Shrawardine Castle

it is fronted by a curving ashlared retaining wall, with a slightly battered plinth and two relieving arches. This may have formed a defensive curtain wall or part of a shell keep, and could be of early 13th century date. On the mound top are wall footings of buildings that once probably abutted against the curtain wall. Semi-circular projecting mounds at the NW and SE corners may mark the sites of corner towers.

To the S and E of the motte is a roughly rectangular inner bailey separated from the mound by a shallow ditch and bounded on its E by a 2m high scarp. This scarp continues S to form the E side of the S outer bailey. Excavation has shown that these defences comprised a bank, possibly fronted by a timber palisade, and flanked by a V-shaped ditch 3.6m wide and 2m deep. Pottery finds suggested a 12th or 13th century date.

To the NE of the motte are the remains of a second larger outer bailey defended by a broad spread rampart and ditch, with a probable original entrance on its E side. A series of building platforms and a hollow-way lie to the W of the castle earthworks in the field toward the road. It is tempting to see these as remnants of the "greatest, fairest and best part of the Town burnt for the safety of the garrison" in June 1645.

56. SHREWSBURY CASTLE
11th-17th century AD

SJ 495128. In centre of Shrewsbury at N end of Castle Street overlooking railway station. (*)

When William I ordered the building of a castle in the county town, probably in 1067, the site was well chosen. A commanding position dominating the only dry land approach to the town across the narrow neck of a loop of the Severn. Fifty-one houses of the town had to be demolished to make way for the royal stronghold. It comprised a motte with conjoined inner and outer baileys. No above ground traces of the outer bailey survive, but it was large, more than twice the size of the inner bailey and extending along the axis of what is now Castle Street.

The huge motte still towers over castle and town, rising 11m above the bailey, and over 30m above the Severn to its E. It is surmounted by the quaint Telford designed Laura's Tower of c.1790. Though originally circular, the motte is now 'D' shaped, as a result of a landslip c.1270, when the 'great wooden tower' on it collapsed, and again in 1443. The roughly oval shaped inner bailey is enclosed by a stout crenellated curtain wall of short straight sections built on an earthwork rampart. Though much rebuilt and repaired, some at least of this curtain may date to the late 12th century - royal expenditure on the castle is recorded 1164-5. Also of the late 12th century is the gateway with its little and large round headed openings. The projecting barbican outside the gateway with its

Shrewsbury Castle

twin guardrooms is likely to date from the 1640s Civil War refurbishment of the castle defences. So too does the two-storey rectangular postern gate on the E side of the inner bailey.

The most impressive surviving structure is the Great Hall range, a large rectangular building comprising originally a first floor hall above a tall undercroft. It is flanked by two three-storey round towers which probably housed domestic quarters reached by mural stairs. Both hall and towers are essentially late 13th century, though

remodelled several times since, the hall was heightened in the early 17th century and later restored by Thomas Telford c.1790 as a private residence for Sir William Pulteney.

Following the pacification of Wales by Edward I, the military significance of the castle declined. By 1530 it was said to be "... much in ruine". A brief period of repair and military restoration during the Civil War was fortunately not followed by the usual systematic dismantling. It now fittingly houses the Shropshire Regimental Museum.

57. SMETHCOTT MOTTE AND BAILEY
11th-13th century AD

SO 448993. 5km N of Church Stretton. Smethcott is sign-posted off the A49 at Dorrington. At Smethcott follow signs to church. Earthworks lie in field immediately to W of church and crossed by public footpath.

Of the original site of medieval Smethcott, only the church (rebuilt 1859), and the earthworks of a Norman motte and bailey castle survive. Though small in size and scale, the castle is superbly sited on a narrow ridge-top from which there are great panoramas to the N. The motte stands c.3m high, though it was originally higher, having had its top removed c.1764 when the underlying gravel was used for road

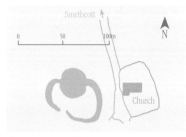

Smethcott motte and bailey

repairs. Today its top is 16m in diameter, and traces of timber buildings on it were excavated in 1956-57. There is no trace of any ditch around the motte base, but excavation has confirmed that it was surrounded by a V-cut ditch. An oval shaped bailey extends S of the motte and its scarped sides stand up to 1.7m high in places. As with the motte there is no surface evidence for a surrounding ditch.

Pottery finds indicate 12th-13th occupation, while records suggest the castle ceased to be the residence of the lord of the manor after c.1272. By 1315 it is said that no manorial buildings remained on the site.

58. STOKESAY CASTLE
13th century AD

SO 436817. 750m S of Craven Arms. Signposted off W side of A49. EH (*)

So picturesque it is almost a cliché, this justly renowned medieval treasure was created in the late 13th century from the wealth generated by Shropshire sheep. In 1281 Stokesay was acquired by Lawrence of Ludlow, the leading wool merchant of his time. He proceeded to build for himself a fine and imposing residence, probably completed by 1291 when Lawrence received a 'licence to crenellate' its walls. More fortified manor house than castle, it was a polygonal shaped enclosure, surrounded originally by a moat, now dry. A principal range of buildings flank the W side of an open courtyard, and all formerly enclosed by a curtain wall.

Visitors enter through an ornate and ostentatious 17th century timber-framed gatehouse that must have replaced a medieval predecessor. Ahead stands the Great Hall range flanked to N and S by two towers. That to the N is the earliest structure on the site perhaps dating from the mid 13th century. It is of irregular shape with a pretty projecting timber turret at the top. Although initially built for defence it was remodelled in the 1280s to provide more comfortable accommodation.

The Great Hall itself is a magnificent structure, complete with fine original cruck roof and wooden staircase. This was the main room of the manor house - the venue for business, meals and entertainment. At the S end of the hall, and accessible only by an external

Stokesay Castle

stair, is the solar block - the private apartment of the lord and his family. Its first floor chamber is lavishly decorated with Jacobean wooden panelling. The 20m high sturdy S tower completes the range. A series of self-contained apartments were contained in its three storeys, and it was perhaps the last of Lawrence de Ludlow's buildings to be completed. No doubt he would have enjoyed the splendid views from its battlemented top. But not for long - in 1294 he was drowned in a "ship of wool" off the Suffolk coast.

59. WHITTINGTON CASTLE
12th-13th century AD

SJ 325310. 3 km NE of Oswestry. Castle is located in centre of Whittington village alongside A495 road. Public car park on N side of castle grounds.

Towers, earthworks and water all combine to make this a visually splendid castle. It is also archaeologically among the most fascinating.

A castle at Whittington is first mentioned in 1138 when it was fortified against King Stephen by William Peverell. In 1204 it passed to Fulk Fitz Warin, whose family continued to hold it until 1420. In 1221 Fulk was given licence to fortify the castle "as much as was essential to protect it from the Welsh". This marked the start of a major remodelling of the castle, and it is to this 13th century rebuilding phase that the surviving buildings belong.

The main feature of the new castle was a rectangular inner bailey encircled by a stone curtain wall with projecting semi-circular towers at the angles. At the NW angle two towers, one still largely intact, flanked a gateway entered via a drawbridge. The drawbridge pit is visible as a recess between the flanking towers. The foundations of a small rectangular keep occupy the centre of the bailey, and those of a hall range against the E curtain wall. There is a well near the NW angle and remains of a circular dovecote at the SW corner. Excavations have shown the keep to have been destroyed by fire in the late 12th or early 13th century and to have surmounted a motte that was later encapsulated within the inner bailey. This raises interesting questions about the motte-like mound a short distance to the W. Recent research suggests it may have been a viewing mound associated with a series of medieval gardens in the castle.

Beyond the inner bailey the principal surviving building is the fine outer gatehouse. Much restored, its twin-crenellated D-shaped towers flank an entrance approached by a stone bridge that spans the moat. A length of curtain wall with two towers extends from the N side of the gatehouse. Extensive earthworks lie to the W including at least two further outer baileys, one containing a fishpond. The castle's outer defences on its S and W sides comprise three concentrically arranged banks, each fronted by a once water-filled ditch. A broad sheet of water also formerly protected the N side. Indeed, perhaps the most striking feature of the castle is the wide-scale use of water in its defences. The moat that survives today fronting the road on the E side is only a small remnant of the once extensive sheets of water that protected the castle.

Whittington Castle

The Medieval Church

Religious life during the Middle Ages has left a rich and varied legacy of buildings and monuments throughout Shropshire. Monasticism, perhaps more than any other facet of this spiritual kaleidoscope can lay claim to having the most impressive tangible remains. Religious communities living a life of religious observance under a form of regular discipline have their origins in Shropshire during the later 7th century. It was, however, during the five centuries following the Norman conquest that monasticism in Shropshire reached its heyday. The myriad of monastic orders found in medieval England is reflected in Shropshire with no fewer than nine different orders of monks, canons and friars at one time represented in the county. These range from the Cluniacs at Much Wenlock with their love of elaborate liturgy and architectural ostentation, to the ascetic and reclusive Cistercians at Buildwas.

None of Shropshire's monastic houses was ever large or of more than local importance. Despite this the county possesses today probably the finest concentration of surviving monastic remains outside of Yorkshire. Even in their ruinous state monuments such as Buildwas, Lilleshall and Haughmond allow a wonderful insight into the functioning of these communities and the religious and domestic duties undertaken by them.

In the later Middle Ages a number of quasi-monastic colleges of resident priests or 'canons' were established in the county. They were private foundations and their purpose was to sing masses for the dead. Of these, Battlefield College founded on the site of the 1403 Battle of Shrewsbury is an especially memorable example.

Frequent visitors to medieval churchyards will be familiar with the remains of medieval crosses, usually found standing on the south side of the church. These somewhat overlooked monuments are commonly encountered in Shropshire churchyards, though rarely as complete as the magnificent example at Bitterley.

Finally, there are the holy wells. They are the medieval expression of a tradition of veneration of watery places that spans millennia. There are many examples in Shropshire, mostly natural springs, often originally enhanced with well-head structures and occasionally with attendant chapels. Today, few show obvious signs of their medieval origins. St Winifred's Well at Woolston is a notable exception.

60. BATTLEFIELD CHURCH
15th-16th century AD

Battlefield Church

*SJ 512172. 4.5km N of
Shrewsbury. Take the A49 N
from its junction with A53/
A5124. After 300m a minor
road leads W under railway line
and on to Battlefield church.
Small parking area at church.*

On the 21st July 1403 the army of Henry IV and that of the rebellious Percy family met in battle 4.5 km to the north of Shrewsbury. It was a bloody affair, and thousands of lives were lost in the ensuing royal victory. Three years later a memorial chapel was founded on the site of the battle. In 1410 Henry IV endowed the chapel as the church of a chantry college to pray for the King and for the souls of those slain in the battle. The college was to consist of a master and five chaplains together with a hospice for several poor persons. A contemporary account describes the site surrounded by a ditch and containing within it the large battle grave pit. Today the surviving remains make it one of Shropshire's most unusual and exceptional medieval monuments. The church cuts a fine figure. Despite heavy restoration in 1861-2, the nave and chancel, both completed by 1409, still retain their spacious, airy, late medieval feel. The tall imposing tower was added later and not completed until the early 16th century. A fine original sculpture of Henry IV looking sternly regal and armed for battle, can be seen high up on the external W gable of the chancel. Of the former collegiate buildings only a fragment of walling remains on the external S wall of the chancel. The large rectangular moat that once surrounded the buildings is now largely filled in, though a partially water-filled section survives, abutting the E side of the churchyard. Elsewhere its course can be traced by shallow depressions and slight scarps. Most impressive of the surviving earthworks is an exceptionally well preserved group of medieval fishponds to the S of the church in the SE quadrant of the moated enclosure. They comprise five interconnected, still waterlogged, ponds, divided from each other by banks, and containing small islands.

Five hundred years after the battle the whole complex remains a powerful and moving memorial to the dead of that long gone summer's day.

61. BITTERLEY CHURCHYARD CROSS
14th century AD

*SO 570772. 5km NE of Ludlow.
In churchyard of St Mary's
church, Bitterley, which lies
0.7km E of Bitterley village.*

Not only the finest medieval churchyard cross in Shropshire but also among the best in the country. This beautiful, elegant cross stands 4.8m high on a tall base of four hexagonal steps. The square socket stone has chamfered corners and an octagonal top. From it rises the slender octagonal shaft which tapers to an ornately adorned cross head in the form of a lantern head. Each of its four sides have ogee-headed niches below gabled canopies, and contain carved, though weathered, figures. That on the W face contains the Crucifixion, while on the E is possibly the Virgin and Child.

Near the bottom of the cross shaft a narrow hole has been drilled N-S through the shaft with a corresponding depression in the base on the S side. Its purpose is unknown. However, some devotees of ley-lines have bizarrely claimed the hole to be a sighting point for a ley-line aligned with the nearby hill summit of Brown Clee. If so, how come the chancel of the church, which pre-dates the cross, blocks the view through the hole? Strange but true. Watch out for those flying saucers overhead.

62. BRIDGNORTH FRIARY
13th-14th century AD

SO 718933. In Bridgnorth on W bank of river Severn (Riverside Road) 300m N of bridge across river.

Until recently it was believed that all remaining buildings of the Franciscan Friary had been removed in the 19th century by the erection of a carpet factory on the site. Then in 1989 sandstone walls were found encapsulated in the factory and subsequent excavations in advance of redevelopment revealed extensive structural remains. Fortunately, much of these have been consolidated and displayed as part of the housing development that precipitated their discovery.

What has been preserved is thought to be a portion of the E end of the Friary church. It is 10m wide, with walls partly standing on and spanning the sandstone river cliff. The internal floor level, of which no trace was found, would have been above the level of the visible wall tops. Hence, the surviving structure must have formed an undercroft, divided into two units by a cross wall which itself may have corresponded with an internal division of the church. Both undercroft and superstructure would have originally extended further E into the present road. The E unit of the undercroft was originally vaulted, as confirmed by part of a vault springer in the SW corner. Access into it was through a doorway in the N wall that in turn led from a stepped passageway running parallel to the building. The S wall of the undercroft is externally buttressed, and includes two large projecting walls that probably served as retaining walls for terraces up the hill slope. All these structural remains are likely to be of late 13th/early 14th century date. In the post-dissolution period the undercroft end unit was remodelled and reused for domestic purposes. A fireplace was inserted in the SW corner, a new door in the SE corner, and the internal walls plastered.

The Franciscan Friary was established at Bridgnorth sometime shortly before 1244 in a typically peripheral location to the town. It was never a wealthy or large house. At its dissolution in 1538 it was described by the Bishop of Dover as the poorest house he had seen, not worth 10s a year and with the houses all falling down.

If, during your visit, you should encounter a tall man dressed in grey habit and wearing a purple cowl, don't be too surprised - its probably 'Old Mo', the phantom friar of Bridgnorth, known occasionally to frequent these parts.

63. BUILDWAS ABBEY
12th century AD

Buildwas Abbey

SJ 643043. 4.5km NE of Much Wenlock on W side of A4169 Much Wenlock - Telford road, 250m before its junction with B4380 (signposted). EH(*)

No monastic ruin gives a finer evocation of the simple dignity of early Cistercian houses than Buildwas Abbey. It was founded in 1135 by Roger Clinton, Bishop of Lichfield, originally as a Savignac house but becoming Cistercian on the merger of the two orders in 1147. In keeping with Cistercian ideals the Abbey was located in a remote, secluded position on the S bank of the River Severn. Its properties were never large and part of its income was derived from tolls for use of the nearby bridge across the Severn. At its dissolution in 1536 the community comprised just eight brothers.

The extensive surviving remains are remarkable in virtually all dating to the later 12th century and few abbeys show such little structural alteration. The church epitomises this. It is austerely Cistercian and magnificent for being just that. An aisled nave of seven bays has plain sturdy arcade piers carrying bluntly pointed arches. The two eastern bays of the nave were separated from the remainder by a pulpitum and included in the choir beneath the tower crossing. The tower itself was low and squat, and still carries the traces of the nave roof line on its W wall. The chancel is short, square-ended and characteristically restrained, with three tall windows in the E wall, and an inserted 13th century sedilia on the S. Both transepts have nicely preserved groin-vaulted E chapels. Only foundations remain of a large 14th century chapel on the S side of the nave. The river to the N dictated that the claustral range be built on the N side of the church. The E range is impressive with its stone vaulted sacristy, chapter house and parlour. The still-roofed chapter house is a treat. Entered through a large

doorway flanked by windows, its floor is five steps below cloister level. A ribbed vaulted roof is supported on four slender piers - two octagonal and two circular, and there is a fine collection of re-set medieval floor tiles. Little remains of the N range which contained the communal refectory. Likewise the W range, where only the cellarage survives of the former lay brothers' quarters.

In the field immediately W of the precinct building can be seen a superbly preserved series of large embanked medieval fishponds. They are a silent reminder that for the 400 years of its existence this was a largely self-sufficient monastic community.

64. HAUGHMOND ABBEY
12th-16th century AD

SJ 541151. 4.5km NE of Shrewsbury. On N side of B5062 road to Newport (signposted). EH(*).

These noble ruins are set in a position of some pulchritude against the wooded escarpment of Haughmond Hill. In this secluded spot a small religious community was established sometime in the late 11th century, to be then formally founded as an Augustinian abbey in 1135. It was the wealthy and powerful Fitz Alan family who were the patrons of this new foundation. Their generous benefactions formed a secure financial basis for much of its ensuing history. Haughmond was one of the larger Augustinian houses and one of the few that could claim abbatial rank. The Abbey was dissolved in 1539,

at which time there were thirteen canons resident.

The surviving remains comprise one of the most unusual and interesting of English monastic plans, arranged around two conjoined cloisters. Of the church only foundation walls survive. Built in the 12th century, it was a cruciform building, 60m long, which, due to the sloping ground, had its E end 4m higher than the level of the nave. An attractive late 12th century doorway at the nave SW corner leads into the main cloister, whose E range is dominated by the chapter house. This late Norman building has a superb triple-arched frontage, richly decorated and incorporating some fine 14th century sculpted saintly figures. It was remodelled c.1500 and the

Haughmond Abbey - the Abbot's Hall

timber ceiling dates to that period.
The S range contained the refectory,
of which the cellar and parts of the S
and W walls remain. Note also the twin
arched recesses of the lavatorium in
the adjacent W cloister range wall.
The rising ground to the E dictated
that the domestic buildings be ranged
around a smaller second cloister to the
S of the first. On its E side are the
fragmentary remains of the undercroft
of the canon's dormitory, with a latrine
block, or reredorter, projecting from its
S end. On the opposite side were the
kitchens and their three huge 14th
century fireplaces are still impressive.

In the 13th century the abbot's lodging
was built on the S side of the little
cloister. It is a two-storey building with
an ornate 15th century bay window
inserted in its S wall. Abutting it to the
W is the 14th century Abbots Hall - a
large sumptuous structure with fine
traceried windows and a twin turreted
gable. It was built over the site of an
earlier hall, the partial remnants of
which are still visible. The abbot's
quarters were converted into
a private house after the Dissolution.
Following a fire in the 1640s this was
in turn abandoned and the site used as
a farm until the early 20th century.

65. HIGHLEY CHURCHYARD CROSS
15th century AD

*SO 741832. In churchyard of
St Mary's church, Highley,
on S side of church.*

A pleasing late medieval churchyard cross
nestling in the shade of a fine yew tree.

The slender octagonal shaft, missing its
head, is set into a large square base that
is unusually and ornately decorated.
Heavy rope-moulding garnishes the top
of the base and there is a carved head at

Highley churchyard cross

each of the top corners - two male and two female. The male heads are flowingly coiffured, while the females are more modestly topped off with pedimented headresses typical of c.1500, which must surely indicate the date of the cross. In the E side of the base is a statue niche, now empty, and heavily embellished with somewhat crude crockets in that charmingly excessive late medieval way. On the S side we find the sacred monogram IHC and a skinny outstretched hand. A chunky three-stepped square basal plinth finishes off the monument.

The church of St Mary is a pretty little medieval building well worth checking out, with a pleasing early Norman nave and chancel and attractive 15th century tower. Shame about the ugly vestry.

66. LILLESHALL ABBEY
12th-16th century AD

SJ 737143. 4km S of Newport. From Lilleshall take road to Sheriffhales SE for 1.25km. Monument (sign-posted) on lefthand side of road at end of access track. EH(*).

The Augustinian Abbey of Lilleshall was founded c.1148 by the de Belmeis brothers in what was then, and to some extent still is, a secluded location in Donnington Wood. Throughout its life the Abbey was plagued with recurrent financial troubles, often exacerbated by religious indiscipline. As for instance in 1518 when the prior was denounced as only 'half-religious' and two canons accused of seeing women of ill repute. When the end came in 1538 the ten strong community were granted generous pensions and the estate and buildings sold a year later to James Leveson of Wolverhampton.

The Abbey was large by Augustinian standards, a fact so evident in the splendid surviving remains. The Cruciform church is 68m in length, and flanked by transepts, each containing two small E chapels. The E end of the church is late 12th century and comprises a choir and presbytery of four bays with a huge 14th century window in the E wall. Stone vault springers at the wall tops show the ceiling to have been vaulted. On each side of the presbytery is a tomb recess, both now empty.

The narrow aisleless nave was completed in the 13th century but cleverly designed to be in keeping with the earlier work. This is best seen in the great W doorway where its Gothic decorative fine detail combines with the by then outdated Norman style semi-circular arched head. In the nave S wall just W of the crossing is the most notable surviving architectural feature - the late 12th century processional doorway that led from the cloister walk. It has design and decorative elements that are repeated in several other doorways. These include the segmental arch supporting a crescent-shaped tympanum and, particularly, the flamboyant use of chevron ornament. Just to its S is an unusual but attractive twin recessed book locker.

Lilleshall Abbey

Of the claustral range the E side is best preserved. Abutting the S transept is the sacristy, originally with an E chapel, later blocked off, and a spiral staircase that led to an upper chamber. Next to it the slype - a narrow vaulted passageway gives access from cloister to the monks cemetery. Then the Chapter House, of which only the side walls and a fragment of window survive - several grave stones, probably of Abbots, are set into the turfed floor. The S range is substantially intact though internally inaccessible. It houses the refectory, later divided into two to create a warming house in the E half. There are only fragmentary remains of the W range which contained the Abbot's hall and private chambers. These were converted into a private dwelling on the acquisition of the Abbey by the Levesons in 1539. During the Civil War, the house was fortified for the King and withstood a siege of several weeks in 1645. It eventually fell after entry was forced through the N transept, hence its fragmentary remains.

67. MUCH WENLOCK PRIORY
12th-16th century AD

SJ 625001. On E side of Much Wenlock, at E end of Bull Ring (signposted) EH(*).

Worth checking out for the fine topiary garden - the squirrel and teddy bear are very cute, the archaeology's not bad either. Wenlock Priory was the largest and wealthiest of Shropshire's medieval monasteries. It was also the most venerable, for on its site had stood an Anglo-Saxon Monastery founded in the 7th century. Little surprise therefore that when Roger de Montgomery decided to found a Cluniac monastery in his earldom some time around 1080, he chose Much Wenlock as the location. Following the supposed finding of the relics of St Milburga at Wenlock in 1101, the priory was developed as a place of pilgrimage. The community comprised some forty monks in the 13th century, though this had declined to less than twenty by 1540.

Nothing is now visible of the Anglo-Saxon church. Of the Cluniac house there are ample and splendid remains, the earliest of which is the Chapter House. It dates to c.1140 and has the traditional tripartite front of central doorway and flanking windows. The elaborately intersecting blank arcading on its inside walls are the architectural highlight of the monument. Also 12th century and adjoining the SE side of the Chapter House is the infirmary, originally a single storey open hall. In the 15th century a large and ostentatious new prior's lodging was built abutting the E end of the infirmary. At the Dissolution both infirmary and prior's house were converted into a private residence and they remain as such today. Standing in the SW angle of the cloister garth is the remains of the lavatorium, where the monks ritually washed before meals. It comprised a circular basin and trough within an

Much Wenlock Priory

octagonal building, which has a circular base decorated by elaborately carved panels. Two of these panels survive. They depict Christ and the apostles, and are among the nation's finest late 12th century sculptures. During the early 13th century the church was rebuilt on a grandiose scale, over 107m long and with transepts over 21m high. Parts of the transepts, W front and nave S aisle survive, but there are only foundations of the remainder. It was clearly a lavish structure, as best seen in the S transept with its lofty proportions and the elegant, lovely first floor chamber at

the W end of the S aisle. The latter housed the chapel of St Michael and was for the prior's private worship.

The end of monastic life at Wenlock came on 24 January 1540 when the Priory was surrendered to the King's commissioners. Twenty years earlier an official visitation had found an alarming decline in morality. The resulting report had recommended that the monks "... Must not take boys to the dormitory ... must not indulge in late drinking ... must not hunt, and their dogs must be expelled from the cloister". Rasputin had nothing on the Wenlock Cluniacs.

68. ST OSWALD'S WELL, OSWESTRY

SJ 284292. On SW edge of Oswestry. Roadside location on S side of Maserfield Road and directly accessible from road.

'St Oswald's Well is a Bow Shot from St Oswald's Church ... there is a Chapel over it of tymber and the fountain environid with a stone wall'. So wrote John Leland in the 1540s.

Unfortunately, nothing remains of the timber chapel, but the well survives. Though heavily restored in 1907, the core of the structure is likely to be medieval in date. It stands at the end of a narrow hollow, and is recessed into the sloping ground behind. The well is a small squared chamber built of coursed sandstone, with a barrel roof, and a roughly carved arched opening at the front. On the inside back wall is a much weathered carved stone head of King Oswald, once said to be 'banded by a royal fillet'. The spring of water rises through the floor of the well chamber and bubbles out through the iron-grilled arched opening.

The St Oswald commemorated by the well is the 7th century AD Northumbrian king who was killed fighting the Mercians at the battle of Maserfield in 642. Many believe this battle to have been fought at Oswestry, with the traditional site being the fields immediately S of the well. Legend tells how after the battle an eagle lighted on the dismembered body of Oswald, flew off with his arm, dropped it, and from that spot a spring miraculously sprang forth. Therein lies the origin of St Oswald's well.

69. SHREWSBURY ABBEY
11th-15th century AD

SJ 498124. On E side of town centre 200m E of English Bridge across River Severn. Public car park immediately S of Abbey Church.

Since its foundation in 1083 Shrewsbury Abbey has dominated the E approach to the county town. Even now, nearly five centuries after its demise as a Benedictine monastery, the Abbey church continues to be the visual focal point of this part of the town.

Following its dissolution in 1540 the Abbey Church was saved for the use of the parish but only the nave, aisles, porch and W tower were retained for this purpose, the E end being demolished. The present short somewhat stunted chancel and transepts were built 1886-8. Much early Norman work survives in the church, with the nave and its aisles largely dating to c.1100. The next major building phase appears to have been c.1360-1380 when the W end of the church was rebuilt. This saw the building of the W tower and its huge and immensely impressive W window, the first two bays of the nave arcades, and the windows in the N and S aisles.

Substantial portions of the claustral and precinct buildings, which lay to the S of the church, survived until their demolition in 1836 when Thomas Telford drove through his new London-Holyhead road. A notable survivor is the refectory pulpit which today stands divorced from the church on the S side of the Abbey Foregate road. Its survival is probably due to its retention and use as an ornamental gazebo in the pleasure gardens that were laid out here in the 16th and 17th centuries. 60m SW

Shrewsbury Abbey - the refectory pulpit with Abbey Church in background

of the church, with its W gable facing onto the gyratory road alongside the railway viaduct is a most intriguing building, known erroneously since the 19th century as the 'Old Infirmary'. It is a late 13th century structure with a first-floor hall over an undercroft, and originally stood on the waterfront of the Abbey's W court. It may have had a dual function, serving as both a watergate and an accommodation block for visitors and guests.

Although only moderately sized by Benedictine standards, and never wealthy, the Abbey was always important locally. By the later Middle Ages it had enterprisingly developed itself into a major pilgrimage centre as the venue for the shrine of St Winifred. In 1416 Henry V himself came here on pilgrimage, on foot, in thanksgiving for the victory at Agincourt. A carved stone panel in the abbey church is the sole surviving remnant of the shrine.

70. WHITE LADIES PRIORY
12th century AD

SJ 826076. 3km N of Albrighton. From traffic lights on A41 at Cosford take minor road E for c.3km. Priory is signposted on lhs of road. Small pull-in area for cars. Monument lies 200m further on at end of track.

The priory of St Leonard of Brewood, generally called White Ladies, was the sole medieval nunnery in Shropshire.
It was founded towards the end of the 12th century for Augustinian canonesses. The convent was always small comprising never more than six sisters, and appears to have had an uneventful history. Following its dissolution in 1536 the priory was incorporated into a large private house. To this house came the future Charles II to spend a day in hiding following his defeat at the Battle of Worcester in 1651, and

before spending his day in the branches of the legendary Royal Oak at nearby Boscobel.

The monastic buildings and the later 16th century house have vanished and only the ruins of the priory church remain today. It is a small late 12th century structure consisting of an aisleless nave and chancel and N and S transepts. The nave is of five bays, with a window in each bay, those on the N side being best preserved. There are doorways at the W end of the N and S nave wall, the N one having its arched head decorated with an unusual but attractive lobed moulding. A fine round-headed arch with scalloped and foliage carved capitals leads into the N transept, which now only survives at foundation level. Of the chancel only the N wall with two original windows remains.

White Ladies Priory - nave north doorway

In the later middle ages a sacristy was added on the N side of the chancel, entered by a now blocked doorway in the N chancel wall. A corresponding building, probably a chapel, was built about the same time to the S of the chancel. Its foundations are visible beneath the E side of the boundary wall that surrounds the S side of the church. This wall bounded a small graveyard used as a catholic burial place until 1844, hence the gravestones against the church walls. The priory's cloister range lay to the N of the church but all trace of them has long since disappeared along with the 16th century timber-framed house which probably stood to the W of the cloister. The ruins now stand somewhat forlornly in a setting still as remote and lonely as in medieval times.

71. ST WINIFRED'S WELL, WOOLSTON
15th century AD

SO 322244. 5km SE of Oswestry. Turn left at the sharp bend on entering Woolston from the S. Follow track for 40m then take narrow path to right which runs past the well house. Exterior visible only. Please respect privacy of occupants.

A delightfully secluded setting combined with the innate charm of its structures make this perhaps Shropshire's most picturesque historic monument. According to tradition it marks the spot where, in 1138, the body of the 7th century Saint Winifred rested overnight during its transit

St Winifred's Well

from North Wales to Shrewsbury Abbey. The well house is a small single storey T-plan timber framed structure with close-set vertical timbers. It is late 15th century in date and probably served as a chapel. Its N gable projects over the well, which comprises a stone built inner chamber with a round headed arch, and within which the natural spring rises. Above the arch is a finely moulded statue niche. The water issues into a rectangular basin lined by large sandstone slabs and with a flight of four steps on each side. Down these steps the devotees presumably descended, either to bathe or partake of the waters. The water then flows through a hole pierced in the basin's downside and into a further stone basin below. This too is accessed by flanking steps and has an aperture in its bottom end through which the water discharges into the stream below.

The well may have been built on the instruction of Margaret Beaufort, wife of Henry VII, who is also known to have re-built the more famous St Winifreds Well at Holywell, Flintshire. Standing by the stream on a still summer's day, one half expects to see pixies and elves frolicking with the dragonflies in this sublime locus.

Medieval Town and Country

Prior to the Norman conquest there was only a single town in Shropshire, and that was the county town of Shrewsbury. During the next two centuries this situation was to be radically transformed. By the year 1300 Shropshire had no fewer than twenty-five places that either were towns or had serious urban aspirations. The reasons for this urban explosion were both economic and strategic. Although not all of these new 'planted' towns were successes, most of the county's present towns do owe their origins to this period. The 13th century saw some of the larger and more prosperous of these towns provide themselves with defences in the form of town walls. While the threat of unrest produced by the Welsh wars must have provided the main stimulus, civic pride and a reflection of status undoubtedly also played their part.

Outside the towns the rural economy likewise experienced a period of great expansion and prosperity from the late 11th to early 14th century. Existing villages grew and new ones were created. Single farms were also carved out of areas of former woodland and heath, and these were often surrounded by broad water-filled ditches. Such 'moated' sites are one of the most frequently encountered medieval monuments in the Shropshire landscape. Their prime function may have been to emphasise the social prestige of the people whose homes they surrounded - be they manor houses or freehold farms.

Regardless of size or location the county's medieval rural settlements were essentially agricultural communities and each would have been surrounded by its arable fields. Today the most tangible evidence of this open-field agriculture is in the form of earthwork ridge and furrow. These deliberately created cultivation strips with their characteristic corrugated appearance are a familiar sight wherever medieval arable land has remained in pasture since its abandonment. Where steep hillsides preclude conventional open fields, medieval farmers often created artificial cultivation terraces. These consist of a long flat strip above a steeply-scarped edge or 'lynchet', often standing to a considerable height. The survival of strip-lynchet field systems over large areas of the south Shropshire uplands, as at Tugford, bears witness to the adaptability and tenacity of the medieval farmer.

The period of prosperity, however, was not to last. An agrarian crisis during the early 14th century prompted by climatic deterioration, harvest failure and livestock plagues was to have a devastating effect on agricultural communities. The Black Death of 1348-9 only compounded the problem. Many settlements, particularly those on poorer lands, either shrank or were completely abandoned. The archaeological fall-out of this decline is demonstrated by the numerous earthwork remains of deserted or shrunken medieval settlements that dot the Shropshire countryside. Sites like Cold Weston and Sidbury survive as vivid reminders of this economically turbulent time.

72. ARLESCOTT MEDIEVAL SETTLEMENT REMAINS AND FIELD SYSTEM
12th-15th century AD

SJ 651008. 2km SW of Broseley. From Broseley take B4375 road to Much Wenlock for c.2.5km. Public footpath leads N from road along track for c.250m to Arlescott Cottage. Where track turns sharply to W go straight ahead across stile and follow path to see lynchet earthworks. To see settlement remains follow track W past cottage, across stream and along path that crosses the earthworks.

In the fields immediately to the E of Arlescott Farm are the earthwork remains of a once larger settlement that existed here in the Middle Ages. First mentioned by name in the early 13th century, Arlescott was deemed to be held by Wenlock Priory by 1484. The earthworks are centred upon a hollow-way up to 8m wide that runs NE-SW for c.150m. At its SW end the hollow-way forks, one branch heading N towards the farm, and the other perhaps originally following the adjacent far lane S towards Barrow. Both sides of the hollow-way are flanked by several yard-like areas containing the rectangular scarps of possible building platforms. Some 50m to the N, adjacent to the farm buildings, is an area of ditches and scarps that may mark the former extent of the farm.

Beyond the main settlement remains, the hollow-way turns N and leads to the head of a small steep-sided valley. At a later date, its hollowed route was used to create a series of ponds, each held by a pond bay c.20m long. The ponds must post-date the disuse of the routeway and shrinkage of the settlement and are therefore likely to be post-medieval.

The N extension of the hollow-way had originally served as a route connecting the medieval settlement to its arable fields. Part of this field system survives as a group of strip lynchets terraced into the NW facing hill slope. There are nine lynchets in all varying from 70m to 110m in length, 6m to 15m in width, and up to 1.5m high. They run along the contours and there are traces of ridge and furrow on the broadest terrace. Elsewhere, in amongst and around the settlement earthworks to the SW are further swathes of ridge and furrow. Most of these cultivation ridges are likely to be medieval, with the exception of two blocks of narrow ridge and furrow abutting the S and E of the strip lynchets.

73. BUTTER CROSS, ALVELEY
13th century AD

SO 752857. 7km SE of Bridgnorth. Take minor road N from Alveley Church for 1.5km. Monument lies on W side of minor crossroads.

A plain, simple, but lovely example of a medieval wayside cross. The stone cross stands 2m high with both shaft and head carved out of a single piece of sandstone. Its square-shaped shaft has chamfered corners, and is set, slightly off-centre, in a circular stone base. The round cross-head has both faces decorated in low relief with a 'Maltese' cross, whose arms expand outwards from a central boss. An inscribed circular border runs round the edge of the W face. At the base of the shaft's W face are carved a 'T' and two 'W's in 16th century style lettering.

The cross has been claimed to mark the site of a medieval open-air market place or alternatively a boundary cross in time of plague. Neither interpretation is likely to be correct. It stands at what is today a minor cross-roads, but which during the Middle Ages was probably of some importance, with one road leading NW to a crossing point of the River Severn and another NE in the direction of Bridgnorth. The cross would no doubt have served as a reassuring waymarker to travellers along these ancient routeways.

74. BRIDGNORTH TOWN WALLS
13th century AD

SO 713930. The Half Moon Battery stands in the private rear yard of 16 Pound Street. No public access but visible from pavement. Town wall at rear of West Castle Street can be seen from public car park at rear of Bridgnorth Library, Listley Street.

The medieval town of Bridgnorth was provided with defences of turf and timber between 1216 and 1223. These were replaced later in the century by a stone wall along much of the defensive circuit. A few fragments of the town walls remain and much of their line can be traced in later property boundaries.

Half Moon Battery, Bridgnorth

Butter Cross, Alveley

of Bridgnorth Castle was deemed officially part of the town and so came under the latter's jurisdiction. Hence from thereon any existing outer bailey curtain wall would have comprised part of the town defences. A short length of this castle/town wall survives at the rear of West Castle Street and can be seen from

the library car park. It is some 6m in length, stands c.5m high, and is built of roughly coursed sandstone blocks.

Murage grants continued to be granted to the town until the 15th century, but by the 1540s it was said that Bridgnorth "used to be strongly walled but the walls are in ruins".

75. COLD WESTON DESERTED MEDIEVAL VILLAGE
11th-14th century AD

SO 550830. 9 km NE of Ludlow. If approaching from Clee St Margaret take the road to Ludlow for 2km. Park on rhs of road 100m after road junction. Walk back along road for c.150m then take public footpath (sign- posted) to SE, parallel to track leading to Cold Weston church. Keep to the path which runs through the site.

Visit here on a cold, bleak winter's day and empathise with the people who 700 years ago abandoned their village, the earthworks of which today forlornly drape the hillside. These remains tell a dramatic story of 14th century decline, dereliction and desertion repeated at numerous places in Shropshire, but nowhere more poignantly than here on the lower slopes of the Clee Hills at Cold Weston.

A solitary cottage and a redundant church are the sole surviving buildings. The tiny church of St Mary, now converted into a private house, is a 12th century structure of nave and chancel. Both church and village appear to have been sited alongside

a principal road running N-S up the hill slope, evident today as a deep and substantial sunken hollow-way. The hollow-way leads SE uphill from the modern road in the direction of the church for c.130m then veers SW, abutting a small disused quarry on its E side, before heading SE again. It is flanked along much of its route by well preserved earthworks. These include house platforms, some with stone foundations showing through, and the scarps and terraces of yards and paddocks.

Abutting the W side of the hollow-way c.80m W of the church is a rectangular depression with internally projecting bank and defined on its N side by an embankment. This may be the former pond of the village water mill, mentioned in the 13th century. From here look S and see the corrugated undulations of ridge and furrow on the pasture slopes. These remnants of the village's open fields were last ploughed in the 14th century, wasted by the climatic deterioration that rendered the thin arable soils barren.

Cold Weston is first mentioned c.1090 but the village withered rapidly during the 14th century. From a value of £5. 3s. 0d. in 1291 it slumped in the space of just fifty years to being worth a mere 4s. 3d. In 1341 it was said to be "… In a waste place. There was once an abundance of cattle there, but they had long been decreasing by reason of the murrain (pestilence) in the district … only two tenants there,

living by great labour and want, and others have absconded to avoid the tax … and the Chapel presented, in this very year, to four Parsons, but none of them would stay". In the face of such a catalogue of calamities it is no surprise that the tenants abandoned the village whose name so aptly reflects its harsh, bleak location on these exposed north-facing hill slopes.

76. HEATH DESERTED MEDIEVAL VILLAGE
12th-15th century AD

SO 557856. 12 km NE of Ludlow. Heath Chapel and earthworks abut the N side of a minor road 1 km NE of Bouldon. A public footpath leads NW from churchyard through the earthworks.

Heath Chapel is the icon of medieval village desertion in Shropshire. It stands

alone and secluded, marooned by the receding tide of medieval agricultural decline. Built some time c.1140 it is the quintessential small Norman chapel - brutal yet beautiful in its simplicity. A plain simple nave and chancel, small windowed and internally whitewashed, is entered through a pleasingly zigzagged S doorway. The chapel has

Heath Chapel

stayed virtually unaltered in these past nine centuries, a stark illustration of the later poverty of the community whose spiritual needs it served.

Probably founded sometime during the boom years of the 11th and 12th centuries the village was located on the edge of the former heathland after which it was named. Its earthwork remains are impressive and extend over 5ha in fields around the chapel and especially in the field immediately to the N. In this field are a number of probable house platforms and the polygonal ditched enclosure of a former moated site, within which would have stood the chief house referred to in 1301. The moat's SE arm cuts across the churchyard and there are building platforms within the moated enclosure, and an outer retaining bank on its W side. A circular stone-lined well abuts the N boundary of the churchyard. The main medieval road through the settlement can be traced as a well defined hollow-way up to 10m wide alongside the field edge to the N of the moat. It heads in a NW direction before curving SW to join with the modern

road. At its S end it runs parallel to a large fish or mill pond, now dry, and which was impounded on its S side by a stout flat-topped embankment some 40m long.

There are further earthworks in the fields to the E and SE of the chapel, and which can be seen from the adjacent lanes. These comprise further hollow-ways, building platforms, yards and paddocks, bounded on their E side by a ditch, beyond which lies ridge and furrow of the once open field system. The sparse historical sources suggest a process of gradual decline and shrinkage of the village during the later Middle Ages. In 1327 there were seven taxable families resident here, but between 1268 and 1407 the value of rents had fallen by almost a third. It was the collapse of arable cultivation in this upland area that probably accounted for the demise of the nucleated settlement during the later Middle Ages. With the move to pastoral farming the remaining families simply upped sticks and migrated to consolidated farm holdings elsewhere in the township.

77. LUDLOW TOWN WALLS
13th century AD

SO 510745. At various locations within the historic core of Ludlow.

Ludlow's town walls 1.5km in circumference were built between 1233 and 1304. They were superimposed on an existing town plan and defensive needs dictated that they were located

wherever possible on the crest of the steepest natural slopes. As a result streets and burgage plots were truncated, and formerly integral parts of the town transformed into extra-mural suburbs.

Most of the defensive circuit still survives, though much rebuilt and

Ludlow Town Wall on east side of Mill Street

repaired. Generally the original walling is, where visible, of a local shaley rubble fabric on the outcropping bedrock. It was fronted by a ditch, now completely in-filled. Later buildings and vegetation now obscure much of the wall, but three stretches in particular are worth checking out. On the S side of the circuit there is a good section running parallel to the N side of St John's Road as far as its junction with Old Street. Here the wall stands up to 8m high in places and incorporates three large brick vaulted openings, possibly former lime kilns. Further W a 40m length of wall with patches of brick repair extends E from the site of the Mill Street Gate. The N circuit is best seen from Upper Linney where it runs E-W

along the crest of the escarpment till its junction with the castle. It stands up to 10m high here, towering over and behind the 18th century and later houses that abut its base.

The walls were breached by seven gateways, but only Broad Gate at the bottom of Broad Street remains. The surviving late 13th century gatehouse is partially built over by 16th-18th century domestic additions. Its twin projecting drum towers though are clearly evident, as is the original entrance passage complete with portcullis arch and blocked arrow slits. This gateway was the principal point of entry into the town from the S and must have made an impressive show of civic pride.

78. PANSON MOAT
13th century AD

SJ 448093. 4km SW of Shrewsbury. From Hanwood follow path S of church, cross river bridge, then path SE uphill for c.500m till junction with path leading N and from which moat is visible 100m further on.

One of only a handful of Shropshire moated sites that is circular in shape. It measures c.38m in diameter with the island raised c.1.5m above the surrounding ground level.

The encircling moat is water-filled except on the SE where there is some in-filling and an outer retaining bank bounds its N side. A shallow hollow-way approaches the moat from the S and leads to an original causeway crossing of the ditch. Scattered brickwork and concrete floors on the island are the remains of early 19th century cottages that stood here till

their demolition in 1964, and which in their turn had replaced an earlier house. Running from the SW arc of the moat is a narrow channel leading to an oval depression in the angle of the field. This may be a fishpond with a feeder leet from the moat. Traces of ridge and furrow are evident in the pasture fields to the S and E.

The moat at Panson is one of a number hereabouts, all of which probably originated as assarting settlements carved out of this formerly heavily wooded area in the 12th or 13th centuries. Panson itself is first recorded in 1429 when it was reputed to be a manor. The moat remained filled until 1964 when contamination of the water supply rendered it untenable. The only surviving building is a brick barn a short distance E of the moat, which was incredulously described as a shop in 1840.

79. PULESTONE CROSS, NEWPORT
13th-14th century AD

SJ 745191. In centre of Newport on High Street, adjacent to St Nicholas' church.

Though headless this cross cuts an imposing figure with its fluted square shaft of red sandstone rising some 3m high from an octagonal base standing on four tall steps. It is the town's medieval market cross, and fittingly occupies a position that would have

been central to the original broad open market place of this 12th century planned town. The traditional name of "Pulestone Cross" is said to commemorate Roger de Pyvilesdon, a local landowner hanged and beheaded by Welsh rebels in 1293 while on tax collecting duties in the Principality.

It is said that the cross can invoke ghostly apparitions. If you stand with the finger tips of your right hand touching the shaft, between midnight and 1 am on St Mark's eve (April 25), you will see a procession of all your acquaintances who will die within the next twelve months. Dare you risk trying it?

Pulestone Cross, Newport

80. ST GEORGE'S MOAT
12th-14th century AD

SJ 711108. 1.5km NE of Telford town centre. Public footpath crosses site. Access the path from Watling Street Road, 100m to N, immediately opposite St George's recreation ground.

This medieval moated site was discovered as recently as 1978 while investigating a reported "Roman encampment". Remarkable really, considering that for decades it had been crossed by a public footpath and

lay wedged between housing and a main road on the edge of Telford New Town. Three sides of the rectangular moat now remain, the N side partly overlain by a bungalow and its garden. The moat ditch is dry and averages 7-8m wide and 1m deep. A 5m wide outer retaining bank flanks the S arm of the moat - a necessity on this site as it is situated on S sloping ground. There has been some mutilation at the N end of the E arm where it is crossed by the causeway path that originally

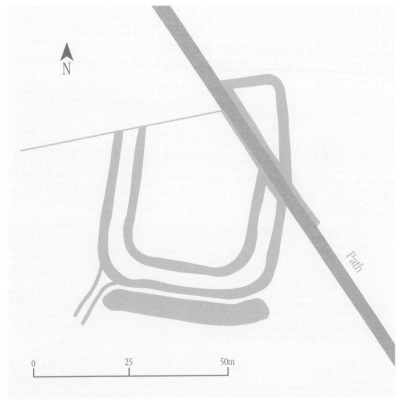

0   25   50m

St George's Moat

led to Woodhouse Mine to the S. A probable outflow leet runs from the SW corner for some distance across the field. Well preserved ridge and furrow can be seen to the S and E of the moat.

This moat probably marks the site of a medieval assart farm carved out of the

'common wood of Wombridge', which then covered much of this area. The driving force behind this assarting was nearby Wombridge Priory, which in 1318 alone had 30 acres of assarts here confirmed by the Crown. Perhaps then, a monastic origin for St George's moat.

81. SHREWSBURY TOWN WALLS
13th century AD

SJ 49001223 - 49311226. On S side of Shrewsbury town centre flanking Town Walls road. Visible from roadside pavement.

In 1218 Henry III ordered the burgesses of Shrewsbury to protect their town with a wall, and by 1242 work was largely complete. The total

circuit was some 2.2km long and for the most part followed the crest of the natural escarpment 'islanded in Severn stream'.

The best preserved upstanding section is that along the curving loop of its S sector where it forms the S side of the eponymously named Town Walls road. Here a 220m length of wall is terraced

Shrewsbury Town Walls

into the top of the hill slope. Although undoubtedly incorporating original 13th century masonry it shows evidence for much rebuilding. Stepped buttresses front the wall at irregular intervals and there is a tall chamfered plinth in places. The wall-walk is partly preserved in a section of raised pavement, but the crenellations that formerly topped the wall were removed in the 18th century.

The one surviving mural tower stands further along Town Walls some 100m W of the end of the visible portion of wall. It is a rectangular structure of four storeys and has a parapeted top. It sits astride the town wall, which it post-dates, and is probably of mid 14th

century date. On its inner side there are doors at street level and former wall-walk level, and small rectangular windows to the upper storeys.

A projecting barbican-like outwork was added on the E side of the circuit to provide defended river access below the castle. This remains as St Mary's Water Lane. Its lower gate still survives as a 13th or 14th century arch, pointed and chamfered on the outside and flanked by buttresses.

In their heyday the town walls must have presented an impressive spectacle stretching unbroken in a great loop above the river. No surprise then that the townsmen chose proudly to portray them on the borough's seal.

82. SIDBURY SUNKEN MEDIEVAL SETTLEMENT
12th-14th century AD

SO 685857. 7km SW of Bridgnorth. The earthworks are in a large pasture field immediately E of Sidbury church. From the churchyard a public footpath leads E across the field.

Sidbury, like so many medieval settlements in the region, experienced a period of decline in the late middle ages. A taxable value of £5. 6s. 8d. in 1291 had fallen to just 21s. by 1341. In that year it was said "there were neither sheep nor lambs therein, because ... land lay untilled, and 13 tenants had quitted under stress of poverty". Even today, Sidbury comprises little more than a church

and two farms. That it was once much larger is confirmed by the earth-works of the medieval village that cover some 4ha in the field to the E of the church.

The earthworks centre upon a hollow-way, up to 8m wide, near the S end of the field. Its W end abuts the track leading to the church and from there runs E for c.150m. A series of enclosures defined by scarps and ditches, and probably representing croft plots, flank either side of the hollow-way. Some possible building platforms can also be discerned. Another hollow-way, up to c.1m deep and 20m wide, runs alongside the hedge on the NE side of the field. Immediately N of the church is the

indent of a large former pond with
an embankment on its E side.
A ditch extends SE from the pond,
but is likely to post-date the medieval
earthworks as it cuts through two
linear enclosure banks.

The adjacent church of Holy Trinity,
though heavily restored after a fire
in 1912, contains copious amounts
of herring-bone masonry in its early
Norman nave. The chancel is
14th century.

83. TUGFORD MEDIEVAL LYNCHET FIELDS
13th century AD

*SO 562872. 13km NE of
Craven Arms. Access by public
footpath (signposted) which is
joined from road to Abdon just
E of Tugford. Path runs parallel
to N side of road, and after
c.250m crosses lower part of
earthworks.*

A fine series of medieval strip lynchet
fields traversing the steep pasture
slopes to the E of Tugford.
They comprise a flight of lynchets
running parallel to each other and
along the contours of the hill slope.
Extending up to c.100m in length
they characteristically terminate
by fizzling out at either end. What
impresses is the height of the lynchets'
steep scarped edges, in places rising

up to 2m. When viewed from the base
of the hill, their serried ranks present
a dramatic sight. So much so that
when first reported to the writer they
were described as the ramparts of a
prehistoric hillfort. Traces of slight
cultivation ridges are visible on the
flat strips known as treads. Gaps at the
E end of the lynchets may mark the
approach ramps where plough teams
would have originally gained access.

Tugford's main area of medieval open
fields lay on the flatter ground to the
W of the village. The lynchets may
date to the 13th century when
increasing land hunger perhaps
forced the farmers into ploughing
these less desirable steep slopes.

Further Reading

Baugh, G.C. and Cox, D. (1988)
Monastic Shropshire.

Beresford, M.W. and
St Joseph, J.K.S. (1979)
Medieval England: An Aerial Survey,
2nd edition.

Burgess, C. (1980)
The Age of Stonehenge.

Forde-Johnston, J. (1976)
Hillforts of the Iron Age in England
and Wales.

Fox, C. (1955) Offa's Dyke.

Higham, R.A. and Barker, P.A.
(1992) Timber Castles.

Rowley, T. (1972)
The Shropshire Landscape.

Stanford, S.C. (1991)
The Archaeology of the Welsh
Marches, 2nd edition.

Taylor, C.C. (1975)
Fields in the English Landscape.

Taylor, H.J. and J. (1965)
Anglo-Saxon Architecture, 2 vols.

Watson, M.D. and Musson, C.
(1993) Shropshire from the Air:
Man and the Landscape.

Watson M.D. and Musson, C.
(1996) Shropshire from the Air:
An English County at Work.

White, R. and Barker P. (1998)
Wroxeter : Life and Death of a
Roman City.

Glossary

abutment - solid masonry placed to counteract the lateral thrust of an arch

ashlar - blocks of masonry cut to even faces and square edges and laid in regular horizontal courses

assarting - the process of clearing or enclosure of woodland waste or common land for agriculture in medieval times

burgage plot - a tenement in a medieval town held subject to customs, rents and services of the borough

caput - the chief place in a lordship, where the court was held

cist - a grave lined with stone slabs and covered by a capstone

claustral - pertaining to a cloister

croft plots - enclosed paddocks behind medieval peasant houses

curtain wall - the wall around the perimeter of a castle or one of its courtyards

crocket - a gothic decorative motif carved in leaf shapes and usually projecting from the angles of architectural features

cruck - large curved timber used for the principal framing of a house

dolerite - a hard dark coloured igneous rock of volcanic origin

garderobe - the medieval name for a lavatory

garth - a yard or enclosure

gullies - narrow linear depressions or channels

hollow-way - a sunken road or track

hypocaust - an underground chamber or duct beneath the floor of a Roman building to facilitate underfloor and central heating

inturned - a method of strengthening hillfort entrances by turning the ends of the inner rampart inwards to form a corridor and placing a gate at the end

lavatorium - a washing place normally placed in the cloister of a monastery and supplied with a piped water supply

lynchet - bank of earth formed over time at the downslope end of a field due to soil movement caused by ploughing

multivallate - defences composed of more than one bank and ditch

murage - a tax to pay for the building and upkeep of town walls

pilaster strip - a narrow rectangular stone column projecting slightly from the face of wall, commonly used in Anglo-Saxon architecture as a structural and decorative device

post hole - hole which once held an upright

pulpitum - the screen that closed off the choir from the nave in a monastic church

putlog holes - holes in a wall which held the timber scaffold poles during its construction

quoins - the dressed stones at the corners of buildings

reredorter - the latrine block attached to the rear of the monk's dormitory in a monastery

revetted/revetment - a wall which supports or retains a weight of (usually) earth

sedilia - seats for the clergy, usually three, in the wall on the south side of the chancel of a church

springer - the bottom stone of an arch at the point it springs from its supports

tympanum - the area between the lintel of a doorway and the arch above it

undercroft - a vaulted ground floor or semi-subterranean room beneath a room above, and often used for storage

univallate - defences composed of one bank and ditch

vicus - a term used for the civilian settlement lying outside but close to a Roman fort

More books on Shropshire's Archaeology and History, published by Shropshire Books

SHROPSHIRE FROM THE AIR
Man and the Landscape
Michael Watson and Chris Musson   £13.99

SHROPSHIRE FROM THE AIR
An English County at Work
Michael Watson and Chris Musson   £12.99

A HISTORY OF MUCH WENLOCK
Vivien Bellamy   £7.95

SHREWSBURY ABBEY
A Medieval Monastery
Nigel Baker   £6.95

SHROPSHIRE IN THE CIVIL WAR
Terry Bracher and Roger Emmett   £10.99

TUDOR SHREWSBURY
Bill Champion   £7.95

THE SHROPSHIRE SEVERN
Richard Morriss   £11.99

PREHISTORIC, ROMAN, ANGLO-SAXON,
NORMAN AND MEDIEVAL SHROPSHIRE
A series of leaflets which fold out into posters -
written by Michael Watson   £1.25 each

For a complete list of Shropshire Books titles contact:

Shropshire Books
The Annexe
Shirehall
Abbey Foregate
SHREWSBURY   SY2 6ND
Telephone: 01743 255043
Fax: 01743 255050
www.shropshirebooks.co.uk